More Than the Sum of Our Parts

A complete guide to understanding dissociative identity disorder and recommended therapeutic approaches.

Amy E. Rouleau, Ph.D.

Copyright © 2025 Amy E. Rouleau, Ph.D.

All rights reserved.

Little Daisies Publishing

ISBN: 978-1-7374594-3-9

Table of Contents

Prologue 3
The Gift of Dissociative Identity Disorder 5
Chapter 1 8
Chapter 2 - Characteristics of DID 24
    The Distinct Characteristics of Each Identity................... 25
    Memory Gaps and Time Loss 25
    Internal Communication and Conflict Between Identities......... 26
    Separate Memories... 26
    Parts 30
        NIS/ANP – TIS/EP Comparison Table........................ 30
    Personality Types 32
    The Host 32
    The Protector 34
    The Persecutor 35
    Child Parts, also known as Littles 37
    The Gatekeepers 40
    The Caregiver as a Compassionate Caretaker............... 42
Case Example #1.. 45
Case Example #2.. 47
Case Example #3.. 49
Chapter 3 - Dissociative Symptoms.................................... 51
    Amnesia 52
        Childhood amnesia 54
    Depersonalization 54
    Derealization 55
    Identity Confusion 56

- Somatic Experiencing 57

Chapter 4 - Diagnosis 59
- Challenges and Controversies in Diagnosis 60
- Symptom Overlap with Other Disorders 60
- Assessment Tools and Techniques 62

Chapter 5 – Etiology 64
- Childhood Trauma Model 65
  - Trauma and Identity Fragmentation 65
  - Developmental Timing and Vulnerabilities 66
  - Neurobiological Underpinnings 66
  - Protective Mechanisms and Coping Strategies 67
- Implications for Diagnosis and Treatment 67
- Specific Types of Trauma 68
  - Emotional neglect 68
  - Physical abuse 69
  - Sexual abuse 70
  - Ritual abuse 72
  - Iatrogenic or fantasy model 75
- Attachment as a Predictor 77

Chapter 6 - Neurobiology 80
- Neuronal Mechanism 80
- Neurobiological Structures and Alterations 81
- Key Brain Regions and Structural Alterations 81
  - Hippocampus 81
  - Amygdala 82
  - Frontal Cortex 83
  - Parietal Region 85
  - Insula 85

    Basal Ganglia 86

    Other brain structures... 87

  Functional Alterations and Identity States................................ 88

  Genetic and Epigenetic Factors.. 88

  Relationship with Trauma 89

  Comparison to Other Disorders 90

  Limitations and Future Directions.. 91

Chapter 7 - Common Comorbidities 93

  Post Traumatic Stress Disorder (PTSD) 93

  Mood Disorders.. 94

  Personality Disorders 94

  Psychotic Disorders 95

  Dissociative Amnesia (DA) and Dissociative Fugue (DF) 96

  Anxiety disorders and dissociative disorders (DDs) 97

  Eating disorders and DID 98

  Substance Use Disorder and DID.. 98

  Conversion Disorder and DID 100

  Challenges in Diagnosis due to Comorbidity........................... 101

Chapter 8 - Non-clinical Therapeutic Practices 103

  Yoga... 103

  Meditation... 104

  Mindfulness Practices 105

  Expressive Therapies 105

  Grounding Techniques 106

  Physical Movement and Exercise 107

  Nature Exposure... 107

  Self-Hypnosis and Parts Negotiation 108

Chapter 9 - Clinical Interventions... 111

Psychotherapy (Primary Component) 111
The Benefits of Therapeutic Alliance 111
Therapeutic Framework: Phase-Oriented Treatment 113
    Phase One: Safety and Stabilization 113
    Phase Two: Confronting and Processing Trauma 114
    Phase Three: Identity Integration and Rehabilitation 114
Approaches to Addressing Dissociative Defense Mechanisms 114
Challenges and Controversies 115
Therapeutic Relationship and Patient Empowerment 116
Pharmacotherapy (Secondary) 116
Hypnotherapy 117
    Benefits of Hypnotherapy for Individuals with DID 117
    Applications of Hypnotherapy 118
    Symptom Management 118
    Trauma Integration 119
    Considerations and Cautions 119
The Application of Internal Family Systems 120
    Understanding Internal Family Systems 120
    The Relevance of IFS in DID Treatment 121
    Direct Engagement with Parts 121
    Resolving Internal Conflicts 121
    Processing Trauma 122
    Promoting Self-Leadership 122
    Why IFS Is the Most Appropriate Approach 122
    Challenges and Considerations 123
Traditional Understanding Identity Integration 123
    Resolution of Internal Conflict 124
    Enhancement of Co-Consciousness and Communication 124

Unburdening and Reharmonizing Internal Systems............. 124
EMDR.. 125
Somatic Therapy for Dissociative Identity Disorder................. 126
  Key Therapeutic Approaches and Findings 127
  Critical Limitations and Gaps... 129
  Future Directions... 129
Cognitive Behavior Therapy for DID Diagnosis 130
Integrative Therapeutic Approach 131
Challenges in Treatment and Diagnosis 133
Factors Influencing Prognosis 134
Therapeutic Interventions and Emotional Regulation for Recovery... 135
Ambivalence in the Recovery Process..................................... 136
Challenges in Accessing Care 137
Limitations and Gaps in Understanding Identity States in DID 138
ABOUT THE AUTHOR... 140
References... 142

More Than the Sum of Our Parts

ACKNOWLEDGMENTS

Thank you, to all those willing to share their lives, their stories, their gifts, and their courage. Trauma has not been the end but a way to begin with lessons of compassion, strength, and joy.

Prologue

Dissociative identity disorder (DID) is often viewed through the lens of extraordinary human adaptability under extreme circumstances, but it stretches far beyond the realm of pathology. This guide explores identity, memory, and resilience, showing how DID reflects broader human experiences. DID is a condition born of trauma. Its mechanisms, including fragmentation, compartmentalization, and adaptation, are reflections of processes inherent in all of us. By understanding the concept of "parts," the distinct aspects of identity that coexist within each of us, we can gain deeper insights into ourselves and others. This exploration of DID not only unveils the resilience of the human mind but also encourages all of us to recognize and embrace our "parts," fostering self-awareness, empathy, and an appreciation of the complexity of identity.

More Than the Sum of Our Parts

The Gift of Dissociative Identity Disorder

Living with dissociative identity disorder (DID) is often described as a labyrinth of fragmented realities, a condition that brings on profound challenges and demands. Yet, within the intricacies of having several identities lies an extraordinary potential, an untapped reservoir of creativity, intelligence, and innovation. This story is a testament to how DID, far from being solely a burden, can become a gift that expands the boundaries of possibility. DID is not a chosen condition, so why not embrace the possibilities?

One of the most remarkable aspects of DID is the capacity to foster creativity. The presence of different identity states, each with its perspective, talents, and preferences, allows for a multidimensional approach to art, thinking, and problem-solving. Imagine being able to access distinct mindsets, each contributing an unfettered application to painting, writing, or scientific discovery. For me, creativity, embodied in some, but not all, of my parts, has been a constant source of inspiration.

When I reflect on my journey, I see how each acknowledged part of me brings something unique to my life. One part is highly analytical, solving complex problems and running businesses, while another thrives in the realm of abstract art, blending colors and emotions into a masterpiece. Together, my parts form a collaborative system. This interplay has allowed me to achieve breakthroughs in areas where others might see only limitations.

That being said, not all of my parts play well together. The artist parts of me love to create, often at the expense of those who want to work on our career or writing. Sometimes, the push and pull of what to do, when to do it, and the emotion attached to each activity leaves us stalled in a haze of doing nothing at all. The sensitive parts (often the little ones) usually lose the battle over "work or play." Creativity is inherent in children. It is important to

incorporate their expertise of curiosity and creativity in running amok in the business department. Allowing creativity into all aspects of life brings new insight and a fresh perspective.
Often because there are little ones present in those who have DID, curiosity is inherent. Each part of me has its memories, skills, and way of seeing things, which gives me a richer understanding than I'd have otherwise. Being able to view life from multiple perspectives has often helped me find creative solutions and new approaches that I might have overlooked on my own.

For example, during my academic journey, I noticed how different parts of me excelled in specific subjects. One part thrived in logical reasoning, while another had a knack for storytelling and literature. Together, these strengths created a comprehensive and versatile academic experience. That is not to say that having DID while also completing three degrees was easy, far from it. As trauma was being processed, I often missed hours, and sometimes days, due to dissociative amnesia. The professional and academic parts would have to go into overdrive to pick up the slack. Overall, this back-and-forth worked out well, but it was not easy.

Without the constraints of a singular identity, I have found the courage to challenge societal expectations and embrace authenticity. Though I keep my circle of trusted friends small, having parts has allowed me to connect with others. The absence of rigid boundaries between identities has also inspired me to explore unconventional ideas, leading to discoveries that have enriched both my personal and professional life. To be clear, not all of my parts are connected or in communication with each other, but those who are prove to be helpful when challenges arise.

Telling one's story is a powerful act of liberation and healing, not only for oneself but also for others who may feel burdened by their experiences of being a multiple. Sharing my journey with DID has been transformative, allowing me to reclaim my narrative and offer hope to others like me. Through writing, speaking, and artistic expression, I have found solace in the act of creating, as well as in the connections formed with those who resonate with my story.

Through mentorship, advocacy, and community building, I've found fulfillment in helping others realize their potential, even amidst adversity. My experiences with DID have shown me that strength lies in getting to know my parts and allowing them to work together for the best possible life. Sharing this message has become my mission, transforming my personal struggles into a source of inspiration for others.

Dissociative identity disorder is often misunderstood, seen only through the lens of its challenges. Yet, for those who choose to embrace its complexities, DID can become a profound gift, a source of creativity, intelligence, authenticity, and connection. By reframing the narrative and celebrating the unique strengths that come with multiplicity, we can transform what might seem like a burden into an extraordinary asset.

For me, DID has been a journey of discovery, a path that has led me to greater self-awareness, deeper relationships, and more innovative achievements. It has taught me to see complexity not as a limitation but as an opportunity for growth. And through sharing my story, I hope to inspire others to find their own gifts within the details of their lives, proving that even the most challenging experiences can become sources of beauty and transformation.

Chapter 1

Dissociative identity disorder (DID), formerly known as multiple personality disorder (MPD), is a mental health condition characterized by an alteration of identity and memory. Those with DID present with two or more distinct personality identities, we call them "parts," each possessing its own memories, characteristics, and attributes. This alteration, or fragmentation, in identity and memory often results in cognitive, emotional, and behavioral changes. The development of dissociative identity disorder is more than a condition with distinct symptoms; it is the result of extraordinary, often horrific, childhood experiences. It is the natural progression of surviving the unimaginable. Backed by research, accounts from the Stoics to modern psychologists, and *this* psychologist, dissociative identity disorder is a natural development during early childhood abuse, neglect, and chronic trauma. DID means we survived it!

DID is on the most extreme end of the post-traumatic stress disorder (PTSD) continuum. Many psychologists characterize ongoing childhood traumatic experiences as Complex Post Traumatic Stress Disorder, but CPTSD has not yet made its official appearance in the DSM-5 (Diagnostic Statistical Manual, Fifth

Edition).

    Theories about the development of dissociative identity disorder often emphasize the significance of the age range in which the condition emerges, suggesting it typically develops before the age of 9. This aligns with what many psychologists refer to as the "magical age of development" in children, a period marked by intense imagination, fluid identity perception, and heightened adaptability. During this phase, children are naturally predisposed to explore the boundaries of reality and fantasy, engaging in imaginative play that allows them to practice roles and scenarios in an unstructured, limitless manner.

    In the context of DID, this magical age becomes both a vulnerability and a defense mechanism. For children exposed to severe trauma, their extraordinary capacity for imagination transforms into a survival tool. Unable to escape or process overwhelming situations, their minds become fragmented, creating alternate realities or identity states that encapsulate specific memories, emotions, or roles. These identity states function as a way to shield the child's core sense of self from the full impact of traumatic experiences. For example, while one identity might carry the emotional weight of abuse, another may remain untainted, allowing the child to maintain functionality and even appropriately engage socially or academically.

    The magical age of development explicates the interplay between creativity and psychological resilience. For those with DID, it is during this time that dissociation becomes a deeply embedded coping mechanism, evolving from a temporary escape into a structured system of different personality states (parts). This process speaks volumes about the adaptability of the human mind in its formative years. While imagination and role-playing are often celebrated as hallmarks of childhood joy and learning, they can also serve as the foundation for fragmented identities.

This magical period of development highlights the delicate balance between vulnerability and strength in a child's psyche. The same imaginative capacity that allows children to create fantastical narratives in play also enables them to construct protective barriers against internal and external pain.

Understanding early childhood development provides valuable insights into therapeutic interventions for individuals with DID. The core mechanisms of dissociation are rooted in the interplay between imagination and trauma. By tapping into the creativity in early childhood, therapy can focus on communication between fragmented parts and foster healing while building a unified sense of self. This approach seeks to repair the fractures caused by trauma, allowing individuals to reclaim their narrative and identity in adulthood.

As a defense mechanism, dissociation enables a child to protect their core sense of self from the full impact of traumatic experiences. Rather than integrating traumatic memories, they are compartmentalized into separate identity states. For instance, one identity state may hold memories of abuse, while another part may remain unaware of the trauma, allowing the child to continue functioning. This compartmentalization provides temporary relief but prevents the child from developing a cohesive sense of self. Over time, as dissociative coping becomes ingrained, identity states (parts) can become more defined and autonomous, leading to the emergence of DID.

Here are some keywords and definitions that may be helpful before we dive in too far. The words, *identity states, alters, parts,* and *headmates* are used to refer to individual personality states within a person who has dissociative identity disorder. The word *system* refers to the collective experience of those individual identities, parts, alters, or headmates. For the sake of this book, most of the time, we will be using the word *parts* to refer to individual identities.

Neutral identity states (NIS) refer to those parts that hold few or no traumatic memories and perform the daily tasks required to be an effective member of society. These parts are also called apparently normal parts (ANPs). They are performative and allow someone to show up to work, be a mother or father, be a volunteer in the community, or whatever typical tasks are present in their life.

Traumatic identity states (TIS) refer to those parts that hold the traumatic memories. They live in a time and space where the abuse or trauma is happening in the present moment. They have little awareness of the present or future, are triggered easily, and often have somatic experiences related to past trauma. TIS are also referred to as emotional parts (EPs) and were formed out of necessity for survival.

Neither ANPs nor EPs are better or worse; they exist together for the betterment of the whole person. The existence of an individual with multiple parts who are separate from one another and yet exist on one body indicates that **we are all more than the sum of our parts**.

The use of Internal Family Systems (IFS) as a therapeutic approach for individuals with dissociative identity disorder (DID) offers an innovative and compassionate method for addressing the complexities of fragmented identities. Developed by Dr. Richard C. Schwartz in the 1980s, IFS is rooted in the understanding that the human psyche is naturally composed of multiple "parts" or subpersonalities, each with its own distinct roles, emotions, and perspectives. In this model, the self is regarded as the core of one's being.

For individuals with DID, the IFS framework aligns beautifully with the concept of distinct identity states. Rather than viewing these states as pathological, IFS acknowledges them as adaptive responses to trauma, created to protect and manage overwhelming experiences. The approach emphasizes connecting with oneself to foster dialogue and collaboration among the various parts. Each part, whether it holds memories of trauma, functions as a protector, or serves as an exiled headmate, is treated with respect and curiosity.

The application of IFS in DID therapy involves creating a safe environment where individuals can explore their inner world without fear or judgment. Therapists work closely with clients to identify and understand the roles of each part, uncovering their motivations and the burdens they carry. By allowing the client to take the lead, therapy aims to build trust and communication between parts, facilitating integration or co-existence, depending on the individual's goals.

IFS has shown promise in reducing internal conflict, alleviating symptoms, and enhancing emotional regulation. For many, it provides a pathway to healing that honors the resilience of the human mind, transforming the fragmented system into a source of strength and understanding. The principles of IFS encourage individuals with DID to reclaim their narrative, rebuild connections within themselves, and ultimately move toward a unified sense of self.

Regardless of the applied theory and subsequent therapeutic approach, the therapeutic alliance remains paramount. The therapeutic alliance is the relationship between therapist and client and plays a pivotal role in the treatment of individuals with dissociative identity disorder (DID). For trauma therapists, this relationship is not just a professional connection but a cornerstone of the healing process, built on trust, empathy, and mutual respect. A well-trained trauma therapist holds space for the client, creating an environment where vulnerability is met with non-judgment, and the client feels seen, heard, and validated. Creating a secure environment is vital for fostering emotional alignment, where the therapist maintains a steady state that enables the client to connect with and resonate with their emotions.

When working with individuals with DID, therapists must be adept at navigating the complexities of fragmented identities. Each identity state may carry its own unique burdens, roles, or memories, and the therapist's ability to honor these states without diminishing their significance is crucial. By holding space for each part of the client's inner world, the therapist provides a sanctuary where the individual can begin to explore and integrate these fragmented aspects of self.

The therapeutic process relies heavily on creating a secure therapeutic environment where the client feels safe to express emotions, confront traumatic memories, and engage in the challenging work of integration or coexistence. Emotional synchronicity enhances this dynamic by enabling the therapist to respond to the client's needs with sensitivity and attunement, fostering a sense of being understood and supported. Attunement allows therapists to gently guide clients toward self-compassion, helping them to connect with their core *self*, as conceptualized in models like Internal Family Systems (IFS).

Attunement is a process by which the therapist is firmly grounded in the present moment, allowing the client and all parts that come to the forefront to be energetically held in a nonjudgmental space. Attunement includes controlled breathing, heart rate regulation, and a calm emotional demeanor. The therapist must model a state of calm so that the client can join the therapist in their space. If the therapist is nervous, confused, unsure, fearful, or dysregulated, the client may not feel safe enough to explore deeper parts and life challenges.

Ultimately, the therapeutic alliance is more than a framework; it is a living, evolving relationship that holds the potential for profound transformation. For individuals with DID, it serves as a beacon of stability amidst the internal chaos, offering a pathway to healing through connection, understanding, and the rediscovery of a cohesive sense of self.

Exploring the *self* presents paradoxical quandaries: What is the *self*? How is the *self* created? For those with dissociative identity disorder, the concept of *self* is foreign and without much meaning. There are many selves, and therefore, no one cohesive narrative of the life that has been experienced.

Identity formation begins at conception. The role of genetics is minimally understood, based primarily on evidence from twin studies. The personality and temperament, generational disorder and disease, and physiological framework all begin with mom and dad's contribution to a newly created human being. Yes, I believe that life begins with conception. The merger of mom's 23 chromosomes with dad's 23 chromosomes has created a brand-new combination, never seen or experienced on planet Earth. That newly formed human is unique, real, alive, and separate (though in collaboration with all of creation) from the existence of all other humans.

Genetics are important, but only in the way they are expressed. Genes laid down at the foundation of conception are turned on and off, diminished or heightened, by environment. Human experience begins in the mother's womb. If a pregnant woman chooses to smoke cigarettes, drink alcohol, or even has a high level of the hormone Cortisol, the baby's environment is impacted and has the potential to interact with certain genes associated with addiction, mental health, or growth hormones. Research continues to emerge on the topic of epigenetics (the expression of genes). One area that has yet to be completely explored is how generational trauma makes its way into the process of conception and child-rearing.

In addition to the nature-nurture (genetics-environment)

debate, there are several psychological theories on the formation of the *self*. Sigmund Freud approached identity formation through his psychoanalytic theory. He proposed that identity is shaped by conscious and unconscious processes; he called them the id, ego, and superego. The triad of consciousness governs desires, reality, and morality, respectively. Mastering each stage of psychosocial development, while balancing the id, ego, and superego, is pivotal for understanding early experiences and the development of a cohesive self. His views laid foundational groundwork for understanding how internal and external forces contribute to identity evolution. Essentially, Freud asserted that any conflict between the known and unknown, what one is aware of (consciousness) and what one is not aware of (unconscious forces), is the basis for psychological disturbances and disorders, including what he called hysteria and repression.

Frued's *id*, is also known as the unconscious primal desires that drive thoughts, feelings, and behaviors. You can think of the id as an infant, or more aptly, the toddler who wants what they want when they want it. There is no filter warning them of danger as they mindlessly venture into new territory or run into a busy road. The id runs on autopilot. All of those ridiculous thoughts that come rushing to your mind (mine too) come from somewhere. If you have ever had a sudden thought of committing a crime, slapping a coworker, or saw yourself careening off an expressway overpass, you may have even stopped to think, "What the heck was that all about?" or "That's weird," because your thoughts took a left turn; you can thank your id. Elements of the id running the show in adulthood can be seen in symptoms of pathological impulsivity and a lack of forethought.

The *superego* is the part of your conscious experience (not to be confused with your conscience, which is your own special Jiminy Cricket), but mostly it lies in your subconscious (under awareness), which thinks of itself as the most moral. The superego is your ideal self.

Moral development begins early in childhood and becomes solidly conditioned around age 5. The sense of right and wrong, good and evil, and all the conditioned consequences are gathered from a child's environment. Essentially, parents, grandparents, teachers, friends, and neighbors play a primary role in moral development. When the superego runs off the rails or has complete control, the narcissist is born; the one who believes they have all the answers, everyone around them is dumb, and they are right, no matter the evidence to the contrary. Consequences be damned, they don't apply to the narcissist.

Thank God for the *ego*. According to our friend Freud, the ego is our conscious self (awareness). The ego keeps the id and the superego in check. A well-developed ego is aware of thoughts, feelings, and behaviors, where they come from and how they impact others.

In the context of dissociative identity disorder, if the id, ego, and superego are fragmented due to early childhood trauma, the balance and identity of who one becomes is chaotic, confused, and can be or appear irrational. How Freud described hysteria sounds an awful lot like dissociative disorders. Born of trauma, the hysterical person acts out unconscious or subconscious experiences; memories hidden from the conscious self. Repressed memories that live in the unconscious only rise to the surface when triggers are introduced, prompting the emergence of different personality states, or parts.

We should probably stop here for a moment and discuss the terms of the conscious, subconscious, and unconscious. The conscious is the part of the self that knows it is a self, it is aware, present, and makes intentional decisions. The subconscious is the part of the self that lies just below our awareness, but these memories, feelings, and thoughts are readily accessible with retrieval cues. For instance, much of our memory, or conditioning, remains in our subconscious. If I were to ask you, "What is two plus two?" most of you, hopefully, would answer, "Four." This information was floating around in your subconscious until I gave you a retrieval cue, the question, "What is two plus two?"

The unconscious is the portion of the self that has no awareness. It contains the mental, emotional, and physical memories that have been repressed. Whether due to trauma or simply forgetting, the unconscious holds the keys to the past. It also has the keys to unlocking the parts of oneself that have been forgotten, dismissed, or stuck.

The father of psychoanalysis was right all along; talk therapy and hypnosis are the most effective way to reach and heal the unconscious parts of ourselves. The therapeutic relationship, trust, and nonjudgment are the building blocks of retrieving the past. We will dive into these therapeutic approaches in the coming chapters.

Erik Erikson, another prominent theorist, presented a psychosocial theory of identity development. Erik Erikson's theory of psychosocial development outlines eight stages through which individuals evolve from infancy to late adulthood, each marked by a specific psychological conflict. The early stages, particularly *trust vs. mistrust* (infancy), *autonomy vs. shame and doubt* (toddlerhood), *initiative vs. guilt* (early childhood), and *industry vs. inferiority* (middle childhood), are especially relevant to the development of dissociative identity disorder (DID). These stages form the foundation of identity, security, and self-regulation. When children experience severe, chronic trauma, especially from attachment figures (parents, grandparents, guardians), during these critical years, their ability to resolve these conflicts is profoundly disrupted.

Children developing DID typically encounter trauma during the stages when they should be forming a cohesive sense of self and learning to trust caregivers. Instead, betrayal and harm create confusion, fear, and internal fragmentation. The failure to resolve these early psychosocial crises stunts emotional development and interrupts the continuity of the self. Erikson emphasized that unresolved conflicts from earlier stages persist throughout a person's life, complicating later stages, such as *identity vs. role confusion* in adolescence. For individuals with DID, this stage becomes especially chaotic, as their sense of identity is not unified. Therefore, DID not only arises from disruptions in early psychosocial stages but continues to distort identity formation across the lifespan.

    From infancy, a child's attachment to their caregiver plays a critical role in shaping their sense of self and emotional security. Attachment theory, developed by John Bowlby and expanded by Mary Ainsworth, explores the bonds formed between children and their primary caregivers, which is significant in understanding the origins of dissociative identity disorder (DID). For individuals with DID, early attachment experiences are often fraught with conflict, as the caregiver, intended to be a source of safety and love, may simultaneously pose a source of terror and abuse. This paradox frequently leads to the development of disorganized attachment, the most prevalent attachment style observed in those with DID. Attachment styles set a child up for every relationship they will have throughout their life.

    Before discussing disorganized attachment, let's examine the other three types of attachment. It is possible that different parts of a person can have a different type of attachment style. For instance, a part that was created to handle everyday life and does not carry the traumatic memories of the past may have a secure attachment style. There may be a young part who was developed out of profound neglect and functions with an avoidant attachment style.

    Secure attachment is what about half of the human race

experiences. Secure attachment is developed in infancy through early childhood. It is the experience of knowing that the world is a safe place and constructed through trusted caregivers. There are no perfect parents out there, but there are good enough parents. When an infant or child knows that their needs will be met within a reasonable timeframe, trust develops between the child and caregiver. Where there is consistency of care and trust, secure attachment continues to hold.

Insecure avoidant attachment develops when a caregiver consistently dismisses or minimizes a child's emotional or physical needs, leading the child to suppress expressions of distress to maintain proximity and avoid further rejection. This attachment style forms as a defensive strategy in response to repeated experiences of emotional unavailability or punitive reactions to vulnerability. For instance, when a child is not permitted to have or express their feelings, this attachment style can develop. Common themes include being told you are too emotional, cry too much, or are weak because you show emotion, or that children are meant to be seen and not heard.

As those with insecure avoidant attachment grow older, they often exhibit discomfort with intimacy, excessive self-reliance, and difficulty trusting others. They may struggle to express emotions, downplay their own needs, and avoid depending on close relationships. In adulthood, insecure avoidant attachment can manifest in patterns of emotional distancing, commitment avoidance, and a tendency to disengage during conflict or stress, all of which can hinder the development of secure, reciprocal connections.

Insecure anxious attachment develops when a caregiver responds inconsistently to a child's emotional needs, offering comfort at times but neglecting or withdrawing at others. This unpredictable care teaches the child to remain hyperaware of emotional cues and to fear abandonment, prompting them to seek constant reassurance and attention. As adults, individuals with anxious attachment often display intense sensitivity to relational dynamics and a strong need for closeness and validation. They may cling to partners, worry excessively about being rejected, and misinterpret minor setbacks as signs of disconnection. These behaviors frequently prompt a self-fulfilling prophecy, as their pursuit of reassurance and fear of abandonment often overwhelms or pushes others away.

Disorganized attachment arises when a child is unable to reconcile feelings of fear with the need for closeness to their caregiver. Instead of forming a stable attachment, the child experiences fluctuating states of approach and avoidance, leading to confusion and emotional turmoil. For a child subjected to chronic neglect, sexual or physical abuse, the caregiver's behavior may trigger cycles of intense fear while also being the only potential source of relief. It is a push-pull dynamic of 'love me, don't hurt me.' The dynamic disrupts the development of a cohesive sense of self and emotional regulation, fostering an environment where dissociation becomes a survival mechanism.

In the context of DID, disorganized attachment contributes the most to the fragmentation of identity. The child, unable to process or escape the conflicting emotions tied to their caregiver, may dissociate to compartmentalize traumatic experiences. Over time, these dissociative strategies evolve into distinct identity states, each designed to navigate specific aspects of their environment. One identity state might seek connection and protection, while another might harbor the fear and memories associated with abuse. This compartmentalization becomes deeply ingrained, preventing the integration necessary for a unified sense of self.

Early childhood trauma and abuse contribute the most to

disorganized attachment and are positively correlated with the process of the physical stress response, freeze. When an infant or child is stuck in a perceived life-or-death situation, the nervous system protects the child through depersonalization. The mental separation from the physical body is necessary for survival. The mind goes somewhere; the body remains. Memories are formed in multiple dimensions, sending the trauma to the unconscious, and the escape to the subconscious. With repeated depersonalization, DID is formed; the child survives.

Therapeutic approaches to DID often incorporate principles derived from attachment theory to rebuild trust and foster emotional safety. Trauma therapists work to create a safe and stable therapeutic relationship that mirrors the attachment the individual lacked in childhood. By providing consistent empathy, attunement, and validation, therapists help individuals with DID address the wounds caused by disorganized attachment.

The diagnosis of dissociative disorders, including DID, was first introduced in the DSM-III in 1980, and revised criteria have been presented for subsequent versions such as DSM-5 and DSM-5-TR (text revision). However, DID remains a contentious mental health condition, and myths and misunderstandings surround the disorder. Some critics argue that the condition's emergence is attributable to therapy rather than trauma, an idea related to the iatrogenic theory, which hypothesizes dissociation is due to the suggestibility of therapies, malingering, or false memories. Conversely, the prevailing trauma theory posits that dissociation is the result of traumatic events. *We* posit here that those who have not experienced the phenomenon of being a multiple, have no credibility for asserting falsehood in their experiences. The severity of dissociative disorders, including dissociative identity disorders, is positively correlated with the severity of childhood maltreatment. In other words, dissociative identity disorder is almost exclusively developed due to early childhood trauma.

Studies indicate that individuals with DID report significantly more experiences of emotional and physical neglect, emotional abuse, physical abuse, and sexual abuse compared to individuals with other conditions like PTSD, schizophrenic disorders, panic disorders, and complex partial epilepsy, or control groups. Severe, chronic, and early traumas are considered predictive factors in the onset of DID. The most common hypothesis is that DID correlates with traumas occurring at an early age, typically by age 9, with reported childhood traumas occurring between 0 and 6 years, and average ages of 3 years for physical and sexual abuse. The trauma theory best fits the hypothesis that chronic traumatic experiences have a major role in the development of DID and do not support the idea that DID is the result of an overactive imagination, fantasy, or suggestion.

Research into the brain and neural processes associated with DID has been conducted using various neuroimaging techniques, including Magnetic Resonance Imaging (MRI), resting-state functional MRI (fMRI), and task-related fMRI. Other methods like positron emission tomography (PET) and single-photon emission computed tomography (SPECT), which measure regional cerebral blood flow (rCBF) or metabolic activity, have also been used to study dissociative amnesia and related dissociative states. Areas of the brain examined through studies include the temporal and frontal cortices, the limbic system, and the brainstem. The hippocampus and amygdala have been identified as primary brain areas associated with DID. The brains of DID patients differ from healthy controls and patients with PTSD. Patients diagnosed with DID have demonstrated smaller hippocampi, bilaterally, compared to healthy controls and patients diagnosed with PTSD (without comorbid DID). Emotional neglect may also be linked with dissociative amnesia and have a detrimental effect on hippocampal subfield volume. The amygdala has been reported to be in a state of hyperarousal (overactive) in those diagnosed with DID. While we will dive into the functions of each area later in this book, a brief overview of the hippocampus and amygdala is that they are part of the limbic system and are responsible for emotional arousal, memory, and recall.

    Research methodologies employed in the study of DID and related dissociative phenomena include systematic reviews, meta-analyses, qualitative studies involving interviews and data analysis methods such as framework analysis or narrative methods, as well as case reports. These studies aim to provide a comprehensive understanding of DID's symptomatology, diagnostic criteria, therapeutic modalities, and underlying neurobiological factors. While significant progress has been made, more research is needed as DID continues to be understudied. For readability, all sources have been listed in the reference section.

Chapter 2 - Characteristics of DID

Individuals diagnosed with dissociative identity disorder (DID) experience their condition through the presence of two or more distinct personality states, also known as alters or parts. These identities may have unique names, ages, genders, and personal characteristics, each existing as a separate entity within the individual's mind. When one identity is in control, the person may speak, think, and behave in ways that differ significantly from their primary or host personality. The switch from one identity to another can be sudden or gradual and may be triggered by stress, emotional distress, or external cues that are reminders of past trauma.

During transitions, individuals with DID may experience memory gaps, finding themselves in unfamiliar situations or with incomplete recollection of events that occurred while another identity was in control. This is called dissociative amnesia. For those of us with DID, these transitions can be frightening. At times, parts can take over completely or they 'come to the front' while the host slips behind the scenes. Still able to hear, see, and experience what the 'part' is experiencing, the host is often left incapable of interfering with the part taking control of the body. This experience can lead the host to feel as though they are crazy, out of control, and fearful of being in public when a part emerges and they slip behind a foggy window to observe what is happening.

The Distinct Characteristics of Each Identity

Each identity within a person with DID can have its own distinct characteristics, including personal preferences, mannerisms, voices, and even handwriting styles. For example, one identity may be assertive and confident, while another may be timid and fearful. These differences are not simply changes in mood or behavior but rather reflect separate, autonomous aspects of the individual's personality. Some identities may consider themselves protectors, while others may be childlike, embodying the emotions and thoughts of the individual at a younger age. There may also be identities that are unaware of each other, while others maintain an awareness of the full system of personalities, acting as internal observers or caretakers. Personality states are often nuanced and appear wholly separate from all other parts.

Memory Gaps and Time Loss

One of the most challenging aspects of experiencing DID is the phenomenon of memory gaps or time loss. When an alternate identity takes control, the individual may not be consciously aware of what occurs during that period. As a result, they may find themselves in unfamiliar places, wearing clothes they do not remember choosing, or having conversations they cannot recall. For instance, I had a friend who realized there was something odd happening when he woke up and his kitchen was full of groceries. He had no recollection of going to the store, buying groceries, or coming home. He then realized he had lost track of two full days.

Dissociative amnesia can cause confusion, anxiety, and a sense of disconnection from reality. In some cases, certain identities may retain memories of specific experiences, while the primary or host identity remains unaware of them. These memory disruptions can significantly impact daily life, making it difficult for individuals with DID to maintain consistent relationships, work, or social activities.

Internal Communication and Conflict Between Identities

Experiencing DID sometimes involves internal communication between parts, which can range from cooperation to conflict, or no communication at all. Some individuals with DID may have parts that communicate with one another through internal dialogue, leaving notes, or maintaining a shared journal. Internal communication can help individuals develop a better understanding of their condition and may lead to increased cooperation. However, there can also be significant conflict between identities, especially when one identity is self-destructive, hostile, or critical toward themselves or others. Internal struggles can result in emotional turmoil, self-harm, or other disruptive behaviors, making the experience of DID highly complex and challenging, and open to comorbidities like eating disorders, bipolar disorder, or paranoid personality disorder.

Separate Memories

In DID, memory functions in a uniquely fragmented manner, reflecting the complex survival mechanism that it is. Rather than being absent, memory in DID is distributed across different parts. Each part holds distinct pieces of the whole, encompassing specific moments in time, survival strategies, or untold narratives. This phenomenon of memory fragmentation is not merely a psychological occurrence but a deeply embedded neurological adaptation designed to preserve the individual in the face of severe trauma. For instance, if a child is being assaulted, her body's response system ultimately goes into *freeze* mode. The parasympathetic response to a life-or-death situation is normal, adaptive, and typical in children. They have no way of escape except through their mind. The deeply encoded memory of trauma becomes trapped in the unconscious, inaccessible to the child's main personality part. What she may remember is the feeling of floating, melting into the flowers on the wallpaper, or the texture of a bed sheet. Her memory recall is fragmented, and when she sees the same pattern of wallpaper as an adult, her body reacts without warning into the freeze response. Her body remembers. If the experience led to the development of a separate part, the sight of the same flowers may trigger the part to come to the front in an effort to survive the moment, even though the moment has long passed. That young, traumatized part lives on in the present moment of when the trauma occurred, not as time exists in present-day terms. What the little girl part remembers is the trauma, a post-traumatic re-experiencing. What the adult woman experiences is a flashback, little glimpses of events in the mind and body.

Memory within DID often operates on a state-dependent basis. Altered states of consciousness specific to each part determine the accessibility of information. For instance, an event encoded by one identity may remain inaccessible to another unless the originating state is reactivated. Separation is evident in cases where one part vividly recalls a traumatic experience, while another, such as the host personality, remains entirely unaware. Neurological studies, including functional MRI and PET scans, have demonstrated that different parts exhibit distinct patterns of brain activation, further underlining the state-specific nature of memory encoding and recall.

Within the DID system, memory accessibility varies, presenting as mutual amnesia, one-way amnesia, or co-consciousness. In mutual amnesia, parts are unaware of each other's existence or experiences, a scenario commonly observed in the early stages of treatment. One-way amnesia occurs when one part, often the host, is unaware of another, while the secondary part retains full knowledge of the host. Co-consciousness, on the other hand, allows shared memory streams or the observation of actions between parts. Varying dynamics of conscious awareness, or unawareness, create a fragmented life story for individuals with DID, complicating their perception of a cohesive self. Their lives are broken into pieces, shared by different identities, events, and relationships.

A particularly significant aspect of DID is the role of emotional parts (EPs). These parts carry the burden of traumatic memories, often re-experiencing them as vivid flashbacks, nightmares, or sensory (body) reenactments. They are integral to the survival of the system, containing the trauma so that other parts can function in daily life. Despite the pain, these memory holders act as protectors, safeguarding other parts of the system from being overwhelmed by the trauma.

Therapeutic interventions in DID aim not at forcing memory recall but at fostering safety, consent, and gradual integration. By increasing communication between identities, reducing the fear associated with trauma material, and helping the host part tolerate memories previously held by others, therapy seeks to shift memories from being dissociated and sensory-based to becoming part of a coherent autobiographical story. Building trust within the system, facilitating internal cooperation, and employing gentle exposure techniques are pivotal in this process.

In essence, the memory dynamics of dissociative identity disorder highlight a profound interaction between psychological resilience and neurological adaptation. Far from being mere fragmentation, the brain has an extraordinary capacity to protect and sustain life amidst overwhelming trauma experience. Understanding this nuanced system not only reframes DID as a functional survival response but also paves the way for compassion and effective therapeutic approaches.

In contrast to the previous statements of complete memory fragmentation, investigations into memory compartmentalization within DID reveal important insights that contradict the notion of fully separated parts with distinct and non-overlapping memory storage. Subjective reports from patients often describe amnesia and experiences of "lost time," particularly regarding autobiographical or trauma-related events. However, some studies suggest there may be covert (under the surface) memory transfer between parts. Even in cases where patients claim full amnesia, experimental methodologies such as free recall, forced-choice recognition, and reaction-time tasks generally show above-chance memory retrieval across identity states.

Studies show that memory gaps aren't completely solid walls but rather partial barriers. While people may struggle to remember information linked to another part, certain unconscious memory processes, like recognizing things they've learned before, often still work. This reveals that memory in DID is influenced more by the mental state and other factors rather than being locked away entirely.

Experiments have shown that people with DID can recall information learned by one part while in another, even if they claim to have forgotten it. For example, tasks that test implicit memory (unconscious or automatic), like recognizing something they've seen before, demonstrate that memories do transfer between parts. The brain uses context, beliefs, and coping strategies to manage the flow of memories between parts.

Parts

Parts in DID can be further disseminated into categories based on their purpose, type of memories encoded, and needed position required for survival. Parts are also referred to as Dissociative Identity States (DIS) and are primarily categorized as: apparent normal parts (ANPs) or neutral identity states (NIS) and emotional parts (EPs) or traumatic identity states (TIS).

NIS/ANP – TIS/EP Comparison Table

Feature	Neutral Identity State (NIS) Apparent Normal Parts (ANPs)	Traumatic Identity State (TIS) Emotional Parts (EPs)
Primary Function	Daily functioning and system stability	Holding and expressing unresolved trauma
Access to Traumatic Memory	Limited or absent; experiences amnesia	Full, emotionally vivid access to traumatic memories
Emotional Expression	Emotionally detached or muted	Emotionally overwhelmed, expressive, often in distress
Memory of Trauma	Avoidant or unaware	Fixated on past events; relives trauma experiences
Somatic Symptoms	Few to none; focused on performance	Frequent (e.g., pain, nausea, tremors, sensory flashbacks)

Orientation to Time	Present-focused, grounded in daily life	Past-focused; often speaks and reacts as if trauma is happening now
Role in the System	Stabilizer, protector of normalcy	Container of unresolved trauma; emotional truth-holder
Therapeutic Needs	Safe emotional expression, connection to internal system	Validation, containment, trauma processing support

In DID, neutral identity states (NIS), also known as ANPs (apparently normal parts) are characterized by a sense of relative stability, calm, and a lack of emotional distress. These states often function in everyday situations without being triggered by traumatic memories or emotional upheavals. Neutral identity states can manage daily responsibilities, engage in social interactions, and maintain a sense of continuity in identity. While neutral states may be aware of other identity states (parts), they generally maintain a degree of detachment from the traumatic emotions associated with those parts. This allows individuals to navigate their lives without the constant disruption of traumatic memories.

In contrast, traumatic identity states (TIS), also known as EPs (emotional parts) are directly connected to past traumatic experiences and are characterized by intense emotional distress, flashbacks, and a re-experiencing of traumatic events. These parts often emerge in response to triggers or stressors that remind the individual of past trauma. Traumatic identity states can be overwhelmed by fear, shame, anger, or sadness, and they may hold specific memories or emotions that are dissociated from the individual's neutral states. These states can manifest as child-like parts, persecutory or protective parts, or any other form that embodies the individual's response to trauma. Unlike neutral identity states, traumatic identity states can significantly impair functioning and may cause distress to the individual due to their overwhelming emotions and fragmented sense of self.

On a psychobiological level, neutral identity states (NIS) and traumatic identity states (TIS) exhibit markedly distinct patterns of activity. NIS are often associated with diminished sensory processing and emotional detachment, enabling individuals to maintain a semblance of normalcy. In contrast, TIS show heightened activity in brain regions such as the amygdala and insula, which are involved in emotional processing and sensory experiences. This difference shows how the mind tries to help a person handle everyday life while also coping with past trauma. It finds ways to keep things running smoothly, even when difficult memories haven't been dealt with yet.

Personality Types

Identifying the roles for which each part was created can often be a product of psychodynamic therapy. Not all people with DID have all of the parts and their associated roles that will be listed in this manuscript, but they should be mentioned for better comprehension of the complexities of DID. The roles and responsibilities of each characterized part could be either one that holds traumatic experiences or one that is apparently normal. The function of each part is a consequence of what was needed to survive and thrive at the time of the creation of that part.

The Host

The host in a DID system often serves as the "face" of the

individual, the state most frequently engaged in interactions with the external world. This part is usually responsible for managing practical tasks, such as work, education, and social engagements, and is often perceived by others as the "real" person. Despite this outward functionality, the host may be unaware of other identity states within the system or have limited access to the traumatic memories that the emotional parts hold.

The host's primary role is to ensure the individual maintains a functioning presence in their daily environment. This often involves compartmentalization, where the host focuses on practical responsibilities while other identity states handle emotional, protective, or traumatic material. For example, the host might attend school, fulfill professional obligations, or care for family members, all while remaining detached from the deeper emotional struggles managed by the other states.

One of the defining characteristics of the host is its dissociation from traumatic experiences. The detachment is a survival mechanism that enables the host to navigate daily life without being overwhelmed by the emotional complexities of unresolved trauma. Hosts may experience partial or complete amnesia regarding their past or may redirect conversations away from topics that could trigger distress. Avoidance, particularly in therapy, is not resistance to healing but rather part of the protective design of the DID system.

While the host functions as the primary identity in external settings, he or she often plays a significant role in therapy as a point of connection for other states. The host may help establish a collaborative environment within the system, fostering communication among the various parts. This unification process is essential for integrating traumatic experiences and developing coping strategies that benefit the individual's system.

Being the focal identity state comes with unique challenges.

Hosts frequently encounter confusion or distress when confronted with evidence of other identity states, such as unfamiliar handwriting, unexplained actions, or sudden emotional shifts. These moments can lead to feelings of disorientation, anxiety, or frustration; this is generally how they find themselves in therapy. The host may grapple with a sense of responsibility for maintaining the individual's external stability, even when internal dynamics are chaotic. Taking on so much responsibility can leave the host feeling worn out, which is why it's important for them to practice self-care and get help from a therapist. In therapy, professionals help the host better understand their role and encourage teamwork with the other parts. By seeing the host's protective role in a positive light, therapy can help the person heal while still keeping their day-to-day life stable.

The Protector

The protector plays a pivotal role in ensuring stability and shielding the person from overwhelming emotional or psychological distress. Protectors may manifest in different ways, depending on whether the protector operates as an apparent normal part (ANP) or an emotional part (EP) that holds trauma. Protective parts, regardless of their classification as ANPs or EPs, serve as guardians within the intricate self-system of a person with DID. These states actively shield the individual from perceived threats, whether external or internal. By mitigating emotional flooding and psychological dysregulation, protectors ensure that the person can navigate daily life while compartmentalizing traumatic material. Protector parts act like bodyguards for the mind. They step in to keep the person safe from anything they see as a threat, whether it's something happening in the outside world or tough feelings inside. By helping to block out painful memories or emotions, these protectors make it possible for someone to get through everyday life without being overwhelmed by the past.

EPs may execute protective actions, such as withdrawing, fighting, or employing defense mechanisms when they sense threats to the system's safety. While these responses can sometimes appear disruptive, they are rooted in the EP's role as a guardian of the individual's emotional and physical well-being. EP protectors may seem unhinged and overreactive at times.

In therapy, the goal is to help the protector part understand what it does and how it fits in with the rest of the system. By recognizing that the protector's actions have helped the person stay safe and stable, therapy can start the healing process. When the different parts learn to trust each other and talk openly, the protector can shift from only reacting to threats to working together with the others, helping everyone move forward on the path to feeling whole and healthy.

The protector, whether an ANP focused on external stability or an EP holding trauma, plays an invaluable role in a DID system. These identity states safeguard the individual from emotional flooding and disruption, ensuring that daily life remains navigable despite the impacts of dissociation and trauma. Through therapeutic support and collaboration within the system, protectors can continue their essential work while contributing to the individual's healing and integration.

The Persecutor

In the intricate and multifaceted world of dissociative identity disorder, identity states serve specific roles that enable the individual to cope with overwhelming trauma and dissociation. Among these identity states, the persecutor part represents one of the most misunderstood and complex functions within the system. Despite its seemingly antagonistic behavior, the persecutor part plays a role in maintaining the individual's survival and internal equilibrium, often embodying the destructive patterns and dynamics of past abuse.

The persecutor part is an identity state within the DID system that is characterized by self-critical, punitive, or aggressive behaviors. This part often copies the words and actions of people who were abusive or hurtful in the past. It does this because, during tough times, learning to act like the abuser was a way to cope with overwhelming situations. The persecutor might cause arguments or pain within the system or in their relationships. Even though these behaviors can be upsetting, they actually come from a need to protect by staying in control, avoiding feeling weak, and dealing with leftover feelings of guilt or not being good enough. In simple terms, this part is repeating what it learned during tough times as a way to keep the person safe, even if it doesn't feel helpful.

In therapy, the persecutor part is often resistant to interventions, as it perceives attempts to dismantle its role as a threat to the system's survival. This resistance can manifest as hostility toward the therapist, sabotage of therapeutic progress, or increased aggression within the system. The persecutor may refuse to communicate openly with other identity states, further isolating itself. Therapists working with DID systems must approach the persecutor part with patience, compassion, and an understanding of its protective nature. It is crucial to avoid framing the persecutor as "bad" or "evil," as this reinforces its self-perception and adversarial stance within the system. Instead, therapy focuses on building trust, exploring the persecutor's origins, and helping it recognize its constructive potential.

Effective therapeutic strategies for addressing persecutor parts involve validation and a nonjudgmental approach. Recognizing the persecutor's role as a protector and validating its contribution to the system's survival can foster collaboration and reduce resistance. Gradual integration, where communication and collaboration between the persecutor and other identity states are encouraged, helps the system recognize shared goals of safety and stability. Exploring the persecutor's connection to past abuse and its internalized messages allows the system to reframe its role as a constructive partner in healing. Addressing feelings of shame and guilt while fostering self-compassion can alleviate their punitive tendencies.

The persecutor part in a DID system embodies the dynamic between trauma, adaptation, and survival. While its behaviors may seem hostile, they are deeply rooted in the protective mechanisms developed during the individual's traumatic experiences. With steady support and patience in therapy, the persecutor part can slowly change and start helping the rest of the system heal and work together.

Child Parts, also known as Littles
Most common among identity states within DID are child parts, often referred to as "littles," which represent an important and distinctive element within the system. Child parts typically embody the developmental stages at which traumatic experiences occurred, reflecting the innocence, vulnerability, and emotional intensity of childhood. Even though child parts may seem delicate or like they don't do much, they actually play an important role in helping everyone understand past trauma and move forward with healing.

Child parts often present themselves as parts with distinctly childlike qualities, such as speech patterns, behaviors, and emotional expressions aligned with younger developmental stages. These parts may range from toddlers to adolescents, depending on the age at which trauma was experienced. They may retain memories, fears, or beliefs from that period, functioning as repositories for unprocessed trauma or lost moments from the individual's childhood.

More Than the Sum of Our Parts

Littles often exhibit a sense of curiosity, playfulness, or creativity, juxtaposed with their emotional fragility. They may express themselves through artistic activities, such as drawing or storytelling, providing insight into their experiences and emotions. Their interactions with the world can be marked by innocence or vulnerability, highlighting the unmet needs for safety and care during formative years. For example, child parts may seek maternal or paternal comfort from trusted figures, indicating a longing for the nurturing they never received.

While child parts may appear vulnerable, they play a critical role in the individual's survival and adaptation. By compartmentalizing traumatic memories and emotions within these parts, the DID system shields other identity states from emotional flooding. This safeguarding role allows the individual to manage everyday life without being constantly overtaken by unresolved trauma. Littles often act as "containers" for pain, keeping it hidden from apparent normal parts (ANPs) who focus on external responsibilities and stability.

Child parts serve as communicators of trauma, bringing attention to experiences that the individual may have suppressed or forgotten. Their expressions, whether through emotional outbursts, detailed recollections, or symbolic art, can provide crucial information for therapy. As they reveal the origins and impacts of trauma, littles enable therapists to address these issues with sensitivity and precision.

One of the primary challenges in working with child parts is their vulnerability and resistance to change. Littles often view the world through the lens of childhood trauma, experiencing fear, mistrust, or confusion in unfamiliar or threatening situations. They may resist therapy or communication with other identity states, fearing that their memories or emotions will be invalidated.

Another challenge lies in their emotional intensity. Child

parts can become overwhelmed by triggers or stimuli, expressing their distress through crying, tantrums, or withdrawal. Their reactions may disrupt daily functioning, creating tension within the DID system. For example, a little might cause emotional flooding during a seemingly innocuous event, such as hearing a song or smelling a scent associated with the traumatic past.

To support child parts effectively, therapists must approach them with patience, compassion, and an understanding of their developmental needs. Building trust is essential; littles must feel safe and validated to engage in therapy. Therapists often use creative and nontraditional methods, such as play therapy, art therapy, or storytelling, to communicate with these parts in ways that are less intimidating.

Validation is a cornerstone of therapeutic work with child parts. Therapists acknowledge their feelings, memories, and perspectives without judgment, ensuring that littles feel heard and understood. By creating a nurturing and supportive environment, therapists help these parts explore their fears and emotions with less resistance.

Gradual integration (linking parts) is another key strategy. Encouraging communication and collaboration between littles and other identity states fosters a sense of unity and shared purpose. Therapists often work to reframe the narrative surrounding littles, highlighting their value as contributors to the system's healing. For example, child parts can act as guardians of creativity or emotional depth, ensuring that the individual retains their capacity for growth and connection.

Exploring the origins of these parts and their connection to traumatic experiences allows for deeper understanding and healing. Therapists help littles process memories and emotions, enabling them to release the pain they carry. This process involves addressing feelings of guilt, shame, or betrayal, which are often internalized by child parts. Fostering self-compassion and providing nurturing care can alleviate these burdens, allowing littles to move forward in their healing journey.

With therapeutic support, child parts have the potential to evolve into collaborative and constructive identity states. They can contribute to the individual's healing by fostering creativity, emotional depth, and resilience. Littles may become allies in therapy, helping the individual access buried memories or emotions that are crucial for growth.

For example, a little who once expressed fear through withdrawal may become a source of courage and insight, guiding the DID system toward stability and integration. By reframing their role as protectors and collaborators, child parts can transition from being overwhelmed by trauma to actively participating in the individual's recovery.

Through compassionate and patient therapeutic support, littles can transform from repositories of pain to advocates of creativity, resilience, and connection. Their evolution reflects the resilience of the human spirit, offering a pathway to wholeness and stability amidst the complexities of trauma and dissociation. By embracing their role and fostering their potential, therapists and individuals alike can unlock the profound healing power of child parts in a DID system.

The Gatekeepers

Gatekeepers are parts that act as protectors and moderators. Like other distinct parts, the primary function of the gatekeeper is to manage the internal dynamics of the system, ensuring that the individual is not overwhelmed by traumatic memories or emotional flooding. They may control which parts take executive control, regulate access to traumatic content, and facilitate communication between identity states. They may act as a filter, deciding when and how certain traumatic content is revealed based on the individual's readiness to process it.

Gatekeepers are often deeply connected to the system's survival instincts. They safeguard the individual by compartmentalizing traumatic memories, preventing them from disrupting daily functioning. This protective role is vital in environments where emotional regulation is critical, such as workplaces, social interactions, or educational settings.

For instance, a gatekeeper might inhibit the emergence of trauma-heavy parts during a stressful meeting, allowing other identity states, such as apparent normal parts (ANPs), to navigate the situation effectively. Their ability to create emotional boundaries ensures that the individual can maintain a semblance of stability and normalcy.

While gatekeepers are essential to the functioning of a DID system, their protective mechanisms can sometimes hinder healing. By restricting access to traumatic memories, they may unintentionally delay emotional processing and healing. Additionally, their intense focus on preserving stability can create resistance in therapy, where deeper exploration of trauma is necessary.

Therapists must approach gatekeepers with patience and understanding, recognizing their purpose while gently encouraging them to relax their boundaries. Building trust with gatekeepers allows for a gradual shift toward collaboration and openness. Communication is particularly important in therapy, where the goal is to create a unified sense of self. Gatekeepers may facilitate interactions between trauma-holding parts and apparently normal parts, enabling the individual to process their emotions without compromising their stability. Gatekeepers are indispensable components of a DID system, embodying the intricate balance between protection and healing.

The Caregiver as a Compassionate Caretaker

A caregiver's primary role is to provide a safe environment that fosters trust, security, and stability. Individuals with DID carry histories of profound trauma, which can leave them vulnerable to feelings of fear, isolation, and mistrust. A compassionate caregiver understands these vulnerabilities and actively works to create a space where the individual feels accepted and valued without judgment.

The caregiver may ensure consistency in their actions, words, and presence, which can be grounding for the individual. Predictability in daily routines, consistent emotional availability, and gentle reassurance can help mitigate anxiety and create a dependable framework within which the DID system can begin to thrive.

Often, parts operate independently and may lack awareness of each other, caregivers can play an important role in bridging the internal gaps by encouraging collaboration and dialogue. By fostering respectful interactions between identity states, a caregiver helps create a sense of unity, reducing internal conflict and promoting emotional harmony. Caregivers might support therapeutic techniques that encourage communication, such as journaling, creative expression, or simple verbal acknowledgment of different parts. Responding with empathy and validation to each identity state's needs, whether it be a trauma-holding part seeking solace or an apparent normal part managing daily life, reaffirms the caregiver's role as a nurturing ally.

Triggers, such as sounds, smells, or situations, can evoke traumatic memories that overwhelm the system. A compassionate caregiver remains attuned to the individual's reactions, offering comfort and grounding techniques during these moments. They may help the individual regulate their emotions through breathing exercises, mindfulness, or simple acts of kindness, like holding their hand or offering soothing words. This support is especially critical in environments that demand emotional regulation, including workplaces or social settings. Here, caregivers act as buffers, helping individuals navigate distress without compromising their ability to function.

While the caregiver respects the protective mechanisms within the DID system, such as gatekeepers and apparent normal parts, they also gently encourage growth and healing. This involves supporting the individual's therapeutic journey, which often includes processing trauma, fostering emotional flexibility, and developing a more unified sense of self. For example, in therapy, the caregiver can act as an intermediary who helps relay the messages of different identity states to the clinician or provide emotional grounding during discussions of painful memories. Their presence offers reassurance, reminding the individual that they are not alone in their struggles.

Therapists must balance patience with empowerment, recognizing the individual's autonomy while offering guidance. DID systems often function with a delicate balance of protection and healing, and therapists must honor this complexity. By doing so, they avoid imposing solutions and instead nurture the system's gradual evolution toward resilience. Therapists encourage the individual to reclaim their sense of agency, empowering them to make decisions that align with their healing goals. Small acts of self-care and independence, celebrated and supported by the caregiver, can boost confidence and foster deeper emotional connection.

Finally, caregiver-replicating identity states may emulate the personalities or behaviors of abusive caregivers. These states reflect the impact of disorganized attachment and unresolved trauma, often mirroring the dynamics of the individual's early relational experiences. Each part has a distinct role in managing the complexities of an individual's lived experiences, particularly those shaped by trauma and dissociation.

Case Example #1

Rachel is a 32-year-old elementary school teacher diagnosed with DID. Rachel's colleagues see her as composed, dependable, and efficient. She manages her classroom skillfully, engages with her students, and fulfills her obligations without outward signs of distress. However, much of Rachel's daily functioning occurs through her neutral identity state, or apparent normal part, which she informally calls "The Teacher." This state is solely focused on practical matters like lesson planning, grocery shopping, and managing finances, shielding Rachel from the emotional turmoil associated with her traumatic childhood.

In therapy sessions, "The Teacher" demonstrates a marked emotional detachment, often redirecting conversations away from deeper topics with phrases like, "That's not relevant right now." When asked about her childhood, Rachel frequently expresses a lack of memory prior to college, reflecting the ANP's tendency to avoid accessing traumatic content. Occasionally, when memories begin to surface, triggered by specific sounds or smells, Rachel might experience physical symptoms such as headaches or fatigue. These reactions indicate the system's attempts to suppress traumatic memories (the freeze response), flee what appears to be dangerous, or fight those nearby as a way to respond to perceived danger. The survival mechanism that was present when the trauma originally occurred tends to be the one that reemerges when retrieval cues (triggers) activate traumatic memories.

Rachel sometimes discovers unfamiliar drawings in her sketchbook or notes in handwriting she does not recognize, revealing moments when other identity states have taken over. Despite this, "The Teacher" continues to serve her protective function, allowing Rachel to maintain her role as an educator without succumbing to emotional dysregulation. While it lacks emotional depth, this part is vital in enabling Rachel to navigate her

daily life with a semblance of normalcy and stability.
Protective Function

The apparent normal part serves as a protective function, ensuring that Rachel remains externally functional and emotionally flat in environments where emotional flooding could disrupt her stability. Although this state lacks emotional richness or connection, it enables her to maintain employment and avoid the intense dysregulation that other trauma-related parts of her identity might experience.

In therapy, the clinician recognizes that "The Teacher" is not resisting healing but is designed to protect Rachel from being overwhelmed. This state functions almost like a gatekeeper, avoiding traumatic material to preserve equilibrium in daily life. Over time, the therapeutic goal is not to dismantle this identity state but to encourage communication between parts, use the strengths of the apparent normal part and other parts of Rachel's internal system, encouraging emotional flexibility, trauma processing, and eventually, more unified self-awareness.

Case Example #2

Consider the case of Emily, a 25-year-old artist diagnosed with dissociative identity disorder. While Emily generally presents as quiet and reserved, her therapist has identified one of her emotional parts (EPs), which Emily calls "Rose." This EP holds painful and vivid memories of her childhood trauma, including sexual and emotional abuse.

"Rose" emerges when Emily encounters triggers tied to her trauma, such as the sound of breaking glass, a smell reminiscent of her childhood home, or phrases spoken in a particular tone. Unlike the apparent normal parts that prioritize detachment for daily functioning, Rose vividly recalls and relives Emily's traumatic experiences. When Rose is present, Emily's demeanor changes drastically. Her posture becomes tense, her gaze distant, and her voice quivers.

During therapy sessions, Rose often recounts fragmented memories with striking sensory detail, like the texture of a worn quilt she clung to during moments of distress or the sharp sting of cold air in a dimly lit room. These recollections are accompanied by intense emotional reactions, including sobbing, trembling, or the urge to retreat physically. Somatic symptoms frequently surface, such as a tight chest, nausea, or sudden headaches, reflecting the body's response to unprocessed trauma.

Rose carries the weight of unresolved trauma that Emily's other parts avoid; her activation often disrupts Emily's ability to engage with her responsibilities as an artist. However, Rose also serves a critical function: she holds the memories that must eventually be processed in therapy for Emily to achieve healing and integration.

In therapeutic practice, Emily's clinician works to build trust with Rose, acknowledging the EP's vital role in the healing process. The therapist encourages gradual sharing of Rose's experiences, ensuring Emily's other parts maintain their stability while Rose begins to relinquish the intensity of the emotional burden. Through this process, communication between Emily's identity states is gradually established, allowing her to develop greater self-understanding, emotional strength, and progress along the path to healing.

Case Example #3

Ava, a 28-year-old woman with a history of chronic childhood abuse, was recently referred for trauma-focused therapy. She has been diagnosed with dissociative identity disorder. In her therapeutic journey, Ava's case exemplifies the challenges and nuances of working with emotional parts who hold the traumatic memories of trauma, a significant feature of DID.

Ava appears withdrawn during her initial therapy sessions. Although her presenting identity is cautious and emotionally blunted, her therapist notes sudden and dramatic shifts in tone, posture, and emotional state when trauma-related topics are broached. Over time, it becomes clear that Ava transitions into a traumatic identity state as an EP, whom she refers to as "Lena."

Fixation on Traumatic Memories

When Lena is present, there is a noticeable change in demeanor. Her voice becomes younger, strained, and sometimes tearful. She exhibits full access to traumatic memories, particularly involving sexual abuse that began in early childhood. Lena speaks in the present tense, often saying things like, *"He's coming in the room again,"* or *"It hurts. I can't move."* These memories are vivid, fragmented, and deeply emotional. Unlike Ava's primary identity state, Lena cannot distance herself from the events; she is reliving them.

Lena is fixated on the trauma and does not possess the ability to shift focus to the present moment. She frequently repeats the same stories, detailing the abuse with unwavering consistency, even when doing so results in distress. She cannot conceptualize a future without fear and is unaware that the abuser is no longer in her life.

Intense Emotional and Sensory Reactions

During these episodes, Lena exhibits intense emotional responses such as sobbing, hyperventilation, or sudden freezing.

She also shows sensory and somatic re-experiencing, holding her abdomen protectively, flinching as if anticipating physical contact, and reporting physical pain or numbness that mirrors the locations where abuse occurred.

On one occasion, after a session in which Lena emerged, Ava experienced vomiting, tremors, and overwhelming fatigue. These somatic symptoms often follow the emergence of the trauma-holder part and represent the body's reaction to re-living trauma in a visceral, unprocessed state.

Direct Confrontation with Trauma

Lena's existence as an emotional part serves a specific psychological function: she contains and confronts the raw emotional burden of what happened. While other parts of Ava's identity system focus on functioning, appeasing others, or avoiding distress, Lena embodies the truth and pain of the abuse.

Her presence in therapy, while emotionally taxing, is critical. She holds the unfiltered memory and emotional weight that other parts cannot yet bear. With support and therapeutic attunement, Lena's involvement allows for the gradual integration of trauma, transforming overwhelming memories into a tolerable narrative.

The therapist works to ensure that Lena is heard and validated, while also building a bridge between Lena and the rest of Ava's system. Over time, the therapeutic goal is to allow other identity states to acknowledge and share the emotional load, reducing the isolation and suffering Lena experiences.

Chapter 3 - Dissociative Symptoms

Dissociative identity disorder manifests through a variety of symptoms that vary widely in intensity and impact, ranging from subtle disruptions to severe impairments in daily functioning. At the mild end of this continuum, individuals may encounter fleeting episodes of depersonalization, characterized by a sense of detachment from their own body or self, and derealization, where the external environment feels unreal or distorted. Sensorimotor alterations, such as unexplained physical sensations or difficulties coordinating movements, may also present themselves intermittently, often complicating the person's perception of their physical reality.

As symptoms become more pronounced, identity confusion can emerge, leading to challenges in maintaining a coherent sense of self. Individuals often struggle with feelings of fragmentation, uncertainty, or inconsistency in their personal identity. Somatic experiencing, the presence of past trauma in physical sensations, further intensifies the complexity of DID, as the body may echo distressing memories through physical pain, tension, or fatigue, even in the absence of a clear cause.

Amnesia

Dissociative amnesia is a striking psychological phenomenon characterized by the inability to recall important personal information, often related to traumatic events. Unlike ordinary forgetfulness, dissociative amnesia involves a disruption in memory that arises as a psychological defense mechanism. It serves as a way for the mind to protect itself from overwhelming distress and maintain a semblance of functionality.

Dissociative amnesia typically unfolds in response to severe emotional or physical trauma and during the freeze response of the parasympathetic nervous system. When faced with events too distressing to process consciously, the brain may compartmentalize or "wall off" certain memories; it is the primary function of DID development. The compartmentalized memories often remain stored in the subconscious, waiting to resurface under specific triggers or therapeutic interventions.

From a neurobiological perspective, dissociative amnesia involves altered activity in brain regions associated with memory and emotion. The hippocampus is a component in forming and retrieving memories, and may demonstrate abnormal functioning during episodes of amnesia. The heightened activity of the amygdala, a region involved in processing fear and emotional responses, contributes to the suppression of traumatic memories by overwhelming the brain's ability to encode them properly. Dissociative amnesia is both a necessary adaptation for psychological survival and can be disturbing to experience.

Individuals who experience dissociative amnesia may struggle to recall specific hours, days, or even years of their lives. Gaps in memory are typically associated with periods of heightened stress or trauma, during which the individual's mind dissociates from the distressing experience. To state the obvious, missing time can feel disorienting, as a person may struggle to reconcile their present reality with the missing fragments of their past.

For many, missing time arises gradually, often prompted by external cues such as conversations, photographs, or events that elicit vague recollections or feelings of familiarity. Missing time can leave someone feeling confused or anxious when they realize that certain parts of their life are simply inaccessible. In some cases, missing time is accompanied by a sense of derealization, making the surrounding environment feel surreal or disconnected, further complicating the individual's efforts to piece together their experiences.

Triggers such as sensory stimuli (sights, sounds, tastes, smells, and touch), emotional stressors, or therapeutic exploration can occasionally lead to the recovery of lost memories. However, this process is often accompanied by intense emotional distress, as the individual confronts the memories and feelings they were shielded from. The fragmented nature of these recovered recollections highlights the intricate relationship between trauma and memory.

In cases where dissociative amnesia is linked to DID, the experience of missing time may also be influenced by the coexistence of distinct personality states. Parts can emerge to cope with trauma, each developing unique patterns of thought and behavior. During periods when a part is dominant, the host part may be unaware of their actions, leading to gaps in memory and missing time. This phenomenon leads to a phenomenon known as a fugue state.

A fugue state is a profound episode of amnesia paired with sudden, unplanned travel or wandering, often accompanied by confusion about one's identity. During these states, an alternate identity may take control, leading the individual to act in ways that are disconnected from their usual sense of self. A fugue state can result in the person having no recollection of their actions or experiences during the fugue, further reinforcing the gaps in memory and adding to the complexity of their condition.

Childhood amnesia

Childhood amnesia is characterized by an inability to recall significant portions of one's childhood, especially those tied to traumatic experiences. The mind's dissociative mechanisms act as a shield, fragmenting memory and creating barriers between the individual's conscious self and their traumatic past. This does not mean that everyone who cannot recall large portions of their childhood has DID or trauma. Childhood amnesia is a common phenomenon among the general population. However, there are no studies to date that indicate how many people with DID experience this in comparison with the average person.

While common in most, in DID, this phenomenon is exacerbated by the presence of parts, who often hold those childhood memories. As a result, individuals with DID may feel an unsettling disconnection from their formative years, unable to piece together a coherent narrative of their early life. The gap not only impacts memory but also contributes to identity confusion, as only bits and pieces of a former life hinder the development of a unified sense of self.

Depersonalization

Depersonalization is a dissociative phenomenon where individuals feel detached from their own thoughts, feelings, or body, as if observing themselves from outside or existing in a dream-like state. The experience often arises as a defense mechanism in response to overwhelming trauma or stress, serving as the mind's way of creating psychological distance from intolerable experiences. By numbing the individual to their immediate reality, depersonalization can temporarily shield them from emotional pain.

The freeze response, a survival mechanism triggered by

perceived danger, is closely linked to depersonalization. When neither fight nor flight is feasible, the body may resort to freezing, an instinctive state of immobility and disconnection designed to endure the threat. It should make sense then that the freeze response and subsequent depersonalization lead to the creation of alternate personalities that have taken on the overwhelming event. Tonic immobility is not well studied but is understood to be a condition that occurs when the freeze response is in overdrive. Staying in the freeze response too long takes on a life of its own and can turn into a process of psychological and physiological collapse.

When DID is developed, in most cases, children do not have the capacity to engage in their fight or flee responses. They are children, and almost always, their perpetrator is an adult; freeze is the only option. During this state, the brain may dissociate to minimize the impact of fear. Once a child has grown up and the trauma is no longer occurring, episodes of depersonalization often happen when parts are switching positions.

Derealization

Derealization happens when a person feels disconnected from the world around them, like their surroundings don't feel real or seem strange and unfamiliar. Individuals experiencing derealization often describe the world as being distant, dream-like, or devoid of life, as though observing reality through a foggy lens or separated by an invisible barrier. Sensory perceptions are frequently altered, with sounds seeming muffled or exaggerated, visual distortions occurring, auditory or visual hallucinations, and time feeling slowed or sped up.

Derealization typically arises in response to intense psychological stress or trauma and serves as a defense mechanism to shield the mind from overwhelming emotional pain. One study found that the influx of adrenaline on the brain's limbic system and proprioception areas of the brain causes inflammation and subsequently visual and auditory distortions. The researchers of the study called this phenomenon *Alice in Wonderland Syndrome*.

Derealization can profoundly affect the daily lives of individuals with DID. Tasks that require focus, decision-making, or interaction with others may become overwhelming due to the distorted perception of reality. For example, a person experiencing derealization may find it difficult to recognize familiar places or people, navigate their environment, or respond appropriately to social cues. Feelings of frustration, helplessness, and despair are common. The unpredictability of these episodes adds to the individual's struggle to maintain a consistent sense of reality, making it challenging to manage relationships, work, or other responsibilities.

Dealing with derealization takes a lot of effort. People can use simple coping tools like grounding exercises, practicing mindfulness, and working with a therapist to help manage symptoms. These actions can help someone feel more connected to the world around them, reduce the strength of derealization episodes, and create a steadier sense of what's real.

Identity Confusion

The challenge of identity confusion in DID is heightened by varying levels of awareness among the identities. Some individuals may be entirely unaware of their dissociative states, leading to feelings of disorientation and memory gaps. Others might have partial awareness of their fragmented self, which can result in internal conflicts and struggles. This constant tension between competing identities, each with their own perceptions or beliefs, can make even basic decisions or daily routines feel burdensome. As a consequence, maintaining stable roles and relationships becomes extraordinarily difficult.

The emotional toll of identity confusion can be extreme, often severely disrupting social, professional, and personal aspects of life. The sense of internal dissonance can be exhausting. The inconsistent presentation might alienate the individual from others who struggle to understand their behavior.

Somatic Experiencing

Individuals diagnosed with DID often experience a wide range of physical symptoms deeply tied to the disorder's traumatic origins and fragmented identity structure. Body memories frequently include physical sensations and sensory experiences linked to traumatic events. Rather than remembering traumatic events as clear stories from beginning to end, people with DID often experience memories as scattered physical sensations or strong feelings. Body-based symptoms can be distressing but are key to understanding how the body holds on to trauma that hasn't been resolved.

Research shows that somatoform symptoms (body memories) are highly prevalent in those with DID, with about 83% of individuals reporting such experiences alongside other dissociative symptoms. They may include persistent physical complaints without a clear medical cause, such as chronic pain, frequent headaches, gastrointestinal issues, cardiovascular abnormalities, neurological disturbances, or immune system dysfunction. Sleep problems and stress-related physiological symptoms are also common. Conventional medical treatments often prove ineffective. Dissociation itself may alter pain perception, sometimes resulting in increased pain tolerance.

Surprisingly, even events that are emotionally important, but not actually traumatic, can be remembered in a scattered or jumbled way for people with DID. This is different from conditions like PTSD, where dissociation usually happens only with trauma. In DID, strong feelings might first show up as physical sensations, which means the way memories are stored and recalled is more deeply disrupted.

Some people with DID notice strange physical feelings that don't seem to have any clear cause and aren't linked to specific memories. These can include things like sudden pain, pressure, or odd sensations that happen out of nowhere and are hard to explain. Sometimes, people even notice unusual touches, tastes, or other bodily feelings, almost like their senses are playing tricks on them. Body memories can happen no matter which identity is in control at the time, but may be stronger depending on which part is present. Different parts in a DID system can exhibit distinct physiological characteristics. Transitions between parts may result in noticeable changes in heart rate, blood pressure, body temperature, or other sensory-motor responses. In some cases, individuals report a loss of sensation or control over certain body parts, reflecting disruptions in bodily awareness depending on the active identity state. Research findings emphasize that dissociative shifts are not only psychological but also accompanied by measurable physical changes. By paying attention to these physical experiences, doctors and therapists can better understand how identity and memory work together with the body. Treating these symptoms is important for helping people with DID heal and move forward.

Chapter 4 - Diagnosis

The Diagnostic and Statistical Manual of Mental Disorders (DSM-IV-TR) outlined DID through four primary criteria: the presence of two or more distinct personality states, each with unique patterns of perception and interaction; recurrent control of the individual's behavior by at least two of these states; significant memory gaps for personal information that cannot be ascribed to normal forgetfulness; and the exclusion of symptoms caused by substances or other medical conditions. Other associated symptoms include depersonalization, derealization, spontaneous autohypnotic phenomena, pseudopsychotic symptoms such as hearing voices or perceiving influences from alter identities, and various somatoform manifestations.

The International Classification of Diseases, 10th Revision (ICD-10), created by the World Health Organization, is a globally standardized diagnostic system used to categorize medical and mental health conditions. Unlike the DSM framework, the ICD-10 did not explicitly define DID as a developmental disorder rooted in childhood trauma. Historically, the ICD-10 provided a slightly different characterization of DID, emphasizing the apparent presence of multiple distinct personalities, each with its own set of memories, behaviors, and preferences, often distinct from a singular premorbid identity.

Challenges and Controversies in Diagnosis

Some experts have debated whether dissociative identity disorder (DID) is a real condition or if it might sometimes be caused by therapy or influenced by things like movies and TV. Because DID is complex and not always easy to recognize, there's been a lot of confusion and disagreement about how to understand or diagnose it. Popular portrayals, such as the well-known case of "Sybil," have fueled these arguments, leading to professional skepticism and, in some instances, outright dismissal of the diagnosis. Of course, ongoing and past research on DID highlights the unjust dismissal of individuals living with multiple identities.

One big problem is that DID often gets missed or mistaken for something else. Because not enough people know how trauma can affect someone, and since DID has symptoms that look like other mental health issues, it can take a long time for someone to get the right diagnosis. Studies reveal that patients with DID often receive an average of 2.8 incorrect diagnoses before the condition is accurately identified. Delays in diagnosis lead us to believe that increased education and training in trauma-informed care within the mental health field are greatly needed.

Symptom Overlap with Other Disorders

Dissociative identity disorder (DID) shares overlapping symptoms with several other psychiatric conditions, making it particularly difficult to diagnose. Post-traumatic stress disorder (PTSD), for instance, is often considered a milder counterpart to DID, as both disorders originate from trauma. Quite obviously, DID has the presence of more than one personality state, while PTSD does not.

Borderline personality disorder (BPD) is another condition closely linked with DID due to their mutual association with childhood trauma and emotional dysregulation. Schizophrenia and other psychotic disorders can also present symptoms that appear similar to those associated with DID, such as auditory and visual hallucinations. However, hallucinations in DID are typically tied to alternate identities and the experiencing of derealization. This contrasts with the more disorganized thought patterns characteristic of schizophrenia, providing a key diagnostic distinction.

Dissociative amnesia (DA) and dissociative fugue (DF) are closely related to, and often symptoms of, DID. Dissociative amnesia, defined by large memory gaps that cannot be attributed to normal forgetfulness, is a hallmark symptom of DID. Dissociative fugue, once categorized as a separate condition, is now considered a subtype of dissociative amnesia and is often indicative of DID rather than a standalone phenomenon.

In addition, evil cousins of DID are depersonalization/derealization disorder (DPD), which shares some symptoms with DID. However, DPD is less commonly associated with extensive childhood trauma, which is a defining feature of DID. This difference between DPD and DID shows how complicated dissociative identity disorder is, and highlights why doctors need to use a careful and thoughtful approach when diagnosing it.

One challenge in diagnosis had been when it came to switching between parts. Earlier diagnostic frameworks required direct observation of distinct personality states taking control of behavior, which is relatively rare. Research shows that only a small proportion of DID cases exhibit outwardly observable switching during interviews. Updated DSM-5 guidelines now allow for inferential and collateral evidence, recognizing that direct observation is not always feasible.

Another challenge in the diagnosis of those with DID is the subjectivity that comes with self-reporting. Patients' perceptions of their DID often vary significantly, influenced by cultural backgrounds and personal beliefs. Trauma histories may be underreported due to shame, stigma, or dissociative mechanisms, further complicating accurate diagnosis. Additionally, professional skepticism can severely undermine patients' fragile sense of self, exacerbating their psychological distress. One of the biggest hurdles to self-disclosure is the flat-out rejection of childhood abuse, or the severity of it, because the part who often seeks treatment is not the part(s) that endured the trauma. Denial is common and serves as a protective mechanism for the whole system.

Assessment Tools and Techniques

Diagnosing dissociative identity disorder necessitates the utilization of a multimodal approach. The multimodal approach often combines clinical observations, psychometric evaluations, and, in some cases, neuroimaging to ensure accuracy and reliability. Below are the primary tools frequently employed in the diagnostic process.

The Structured Clinical Interview for DSM-IV Dissociative Disorders (SCID-D) is a clinician-administered evaluation specifically designed to assess a range of dissociative symptoms, such as depersonalization, derealization, dissociative amnesia, and identity alteration or confusion. This tool is consistent in scoring across administrators and settings. In other words, it is a valid test for assessing DID and distinguishing dissociative disorders from psychotic conditions.

Another valuable instrument is the Dissociative Disorders Interview Schedule (DDIS). This structured interview assesses not only DID but also associated features, including the individual's history of childhood trauma. As a comprehensive measure of pathological dissociation, the DDIS offers critical insights into the broader context of a patient's experiences.

The Multidimensional Inventory of Dissociation (MID) serves

as a thorough diagnostic self-report inventory, providing clinicians with a detailed assessment of dissociative patterns. When used appropriately, it is highly accurate in confirming a DID diagnosis.

For screening purposes, the Dissociative Experiences Scale (DES-II) is a widely adopted self-report measure. It evaluates the frequency of cognitive-emotional dissociative phenomena, including symptoms such as amnesia, depersonalization, derealization, and imagination/absorption. While it is a useful preliminary tool, it is important to note that the DES-II alone cannot validate a clinical diagnosis. A more focused variant, the DES-T (Dissociative Taxon), is tailored to assess the pathological indicators of dissociation in greater depth.

Collectively, these tools form an essential framework for the comprehensive evaluation and diagnosis of dissociative identity disorder, ensuring that clinical assessments are both nuanced and evidence-based. If you are a clinician (therapist, psychologist, psychiatrist, etc.) it is best to get a baseline by administering these tools early in the relationship and then administer the same assessments after some time (1-3 months) when the therapeutic relationship has been built up. Administering assessments periodically is a great way to determine if symptoms are reduced, increased, or have remained the same.

Chapter 5 – Etiology

Several theoretical models attempt to explain the origins and mechanisms of DID. The *trauma model* posits that extreme childhood trauma, especially abuse or neglect during early developmental stages, impairs the formation of a cohesive self. To manage overwhelming effects and maintain some sense of psychological survival, the child fragments their identity into compartmentalized states. Dissociation serves as a defense mechanism, protecting the child from emotional annihilation.

The theory of *structural dissociation* further elaborates that individuals with DID fail to integrate conflicting goals, feelings, and experiences into a unified whole. Instead, they develop structurally distinct subsystems of personality, each with their own first-person experience.

Attachment theory also contributes to the understanding of DID, suggesting that early relational trauma disrupts the development of a stable self by fostering conflicting internal working models of attachment figures.

Cognitively, DID can be viewed as a failure to integrate psychological modes, wherein separate clusters of memory, identity, and behavior evolve independently. These modes become rigid, enduring systems of thought and behavior that are mutually inaccessible.

Recent research on the brain backs up the idea of dissociation, showing that people with dissociative identity disorder have real differences in how their brains work when they're in different identity states. These differences can affect how they handle emotions, remember things, and respond physically. This means that dissociative states are not just make-believe or pretend; they have real, physical changes in the brain.

Childhood Trauma Model

The trauma model is regarded as one of the most robust frameworks for understanding the development of dissociative identity disorder. This model centers on the idea that severe childhood trauma, particularly during crucial developmental periods, disrupts the natural integration of identity and self-concept. Below is an expanded exploration of this theoretical foundation.

Trauma and Identity Fragmentation

The trauma model emphasizes the role of overwhelming stress and emotional pain as catalysts for dissociation. In instances of extreme abuse or neglect, a child lacks the emotional and cognitive resources necessary to process traumatic experiences. Instead of integrating these experiences into a coherent sense of self, the child fragments their identity into distinct *parts*. Each of these parts serves a specific function, such as holding traumatic memories, managing interpersonal interactions, or providing emotional refuge.

The fragmentation is not merely psychological but also deeply rooted in survival mechanisms. Dissociation allows the child to compartmentalize unbearable experiences, often feeling like a life-or-death situation, shielding their core self from the destructive impact of trauma. Over time, these fragmented states evolve into structurally distinct subsystems, each with their own memories, emotions, and patterns of behavior. Compartmentalization is further reinforced if the trauma is chronic, repetitive, or involves betrayal by trusted caregivers.

Developmental Timing and Vulnerabilities

Early developmental stages are particularly critical. The trauma model emphasized that cohesion of identity requires a safe environment, consistent caregiving, and opportunities for emotional growth. When these factors are absent, particularly during infancy or early childhood, the brain's ability to form unified psychological structures becomes impaired. In such circumstances, dissociation is not merely a reaction to trauma but a developmental adaptation to an unsafe world.

Children exposed to repeated emotional, physical, or sexual abuse are at heightened risk for dissociation. Children who experience things like being ignored, seeing violence at home, or having caregivers who aren't consistent are at even greater risk. These tough situations can disrupt how their brains and bodies respond to stress, making it harder for them to form clear memories and leading to patterns of repeated dissociation.

Neurobiological Underpinnings

The trauma model is supported by research into the neurobiological impact of trauma. It has been found that exposure to chronic trauma influences the developing nervous system, altering brain structures involved in emotion regulation, memory retrieval, and self-perception. Neuroimaging reveals distinct patterns of brain activation associated with identity states in individuals with DID, including changes in the limbic system and prefrontal cortex. These findings validate the trauma model by demonstrating that dissociation is not merely psychological but has a measurable, physical manifestation in the brain.

Protective Mechanisms and Coping Strategies

Another critical aspect of the trauma model is its view of dissociation as a protective mechanism. Dissociation allows individuals to compartmentalize traumatic memories and feelings, creating internal *safe zones* that help them navigate daily life. For a child in an abusive environment, this mechanism can be lifesaving, allowing them to function and interact while shielding their core self from trauma's full impact.

However, as these dissociative states become more entrenched, they can lead to lasting difficulties in memory retrieval, emotional regulation, and interpersonal relationships. The trauma model recognizes this duality: dissociation as both a survival strategy and a source of long-term psychological challenges.

Implications for Diagnosis and Treatment

Anchored in the premise that DID originates from unresolved trauma, the trauma model informs strategies for diagnosis and treatment. It highlights the importance of creating a safe therapeutic environment where patients can explore fragmented identity states without fear of judgment or retraumatization. Trauma-focused therapies such as internal family systems therapy (IFS), cognitive behavioral therapy (CBT), traditional psychodynamic therapy, hypnotherapy, somatic therapy, EMDR (Eye Movement Desensitization and Reprocessing), and sensorimotor psychotherapy incorporate elements of the trauma model to help individuals integrate their dissociative parts and build a cohesive sense of self.

The trauma model provides a crucial lens for understanding dissociative identity disorder as a profound adaptation to early and extreme adversity. By having a clear understanding that there is a strong relationship between trauma, dissociation, and identity fragmentation, this framework not only advances theoretical comprehension but also lays the groundwork for compassionate and effective therapeutic interventions. Through continued research and clinical application, the trauma model remains indispensable in addressing the complex realities of DID.

Specific Types of Trauma

Abuse and neglect are contributing factors associated with the development of DID. While witnessing violence, household dysfunction, and insecure attachment styles are also associated with a DID diagnosis, profound and chronic abuse and neglect are forefront in assessment and diagnosis. Abuse and neglect foster an environment where fragmented identity states serve as a critical coping mechanism.

Emotional neglect

Emotional abuse in children refers to a pattern of behavior by caregivers, parents, or other adults that impairs a child's emotional development or sense of self-worth. Unlike physical or sexual abuse, emotional abuse is often more insidious and less visibly identifiable. Yet, it can be just as damaging, if not more so, in its long-term psychological impact. It includes verbal assaults, constant criticism, threats, rejection, humiliation, isolation, or exposure to chaotic and hostile environments. The harm is psychological, often affecting the child's self-esteem, emotional regulation, and social development.

Emotional abuse is a particularly harmful form of maltreatment because it undermines a child's developing sense of identity, safety, and worth. It is often difficult to detect and prove due to its non-physical nature, but its effects can be long-lasting and pervasive. Effective intervention requires awareness, thorough assessment of behavior patterns, and attention to the child's emotional and psychological well-being, not just their physical safety.

Physical abuse

Physical abuse in children involves the deliberate infliction of bodily harm by a parent, caregiver, or other adult. It includes any non-accidental action that causes physical injury or poses a significant risk of harm. Physical abuse is a serious form of child maltreatment that not only affects a child's immediate safety but can also result in profound developmental, psychological, and neurological consequences, particularly when chronic and severe. In extreme cases, repeated physical abuse during critical developmental periods has been linked to the emergence of dissociative identity disorder.

When a child is subjected to overwhelming trauma, especially trauma that is unpredictable or perpetrated by attachment figures such as parents or caregivers, it can exceed the child's capacity to process or cope with the experience. Physical abuse under these conditions becomes particularly destabilizing, as it not only inflicts harm but also shatters the foundational sense of safety and trust that a child depends on for healthy development. The child's psychological defenses, still immature and forming, are unable to integrate the traumatic experience into a coherent narrative or emotional framework. As a result, the child may resort to more extreme, unconscious mechanisms to survive the emotional devastation.

One of the primary survival mechanisms in such circumstances is dissociation. In the face of inescapable abuse, the child may detach from the present moment, from bodily sensations, or even from their own sense of self. This dissociative response acts as a form of psychological escape, allowing the child to endure situations that would otherwise be intolerable. When these episodes of dissociation become frequent and habitual, particularly in early childhood, they can evolve into compartmentalized identity states.

Physical abuse in children is a traumatic experience with immediate and long-term effects. While the visible injuries may heal, the psychological consequences, especially when the abuse is chronic and severe, can be enduring. In some cases, the child's only means of survival is to psychologically escape, fragmenting their identity and laying the groundwork for dissociative identity disorder. Early recognition, intervention, and trauma-informed care are critical to prevent the long-term consequences of abuse and support healing in affected children. Examples of physical abuse include hitting, slapping, punching, shaking, throwing, burning, scalding, choking, suffocating, beating with objects (such as belts, sticks, or cords), and biting.

Sexual abuse

Sexual abuse in children is a profound violation that affects not only the body but also the mind, identity, and emotional development of the child. It includes any sexual activity imposed upon a child by an adult or older adolescent, including molestation, rape, exploitation, or exposure to sexual content. Unlike other forms of abuse, sexual abuse carries a uniquely invasive quality that distorts a child's understanding of boundaries, trust, safety, and autonomy. Because it is often perpetrated by someone known to or trusted by the child, such as a caregiver or family member, it introduces deep relational betrayal and confusion. Relationship betrayal intensifies the psychological damage, as the child is placed in an impossible position, dependent on someone who simultaneously harms and may appear to love or care for them. This often leads to disorganized attachment.

The impact of childhood sexual abuse can be devastating and enduring, especially when it is repeated, severe, and occurs at a young age. One of the most significant psychological consequences of early, chronic sexual abuse is the development of dissociative disorders. When a child is exposed to overwhelming sexual trauma that they are not developmentally capable of understanding or emotionally processing, dissociation becomes a primary defense mechanism. In the face of pain, fear, and confusion, the child may mentally disengage from the situation (depersonalization) by detaching from the present moment, bodily sensations, and eventually from their own sense of self. Deep detachment from one's physical body allows for the psychological separation of traumatic experiences, enabling the child to function in daily life while isolating the abuse in a separate mental space.

As dissociation continues, particularly in cases of repeated sexual abuse during early childhood, it may evolve into a more structured internal defense system. When DID is developing, the child creates alternate personality states, designed to hold specific aspects of the trauma. One identity may carry the terror and physical sensations of the abuse, another may hold the shame, and another may function in the outside world, appearing unaffected and unaware. These identities can operate with varying degrees of awareness of one another, and over time, they may develop their own perspectives, memories, and roles. Parts are often specific, separate from the host, and serve to preserve life. This means that parts created during traumatic events take on the personality traits necessary to deal with the people who have hurt them, shamed them, and degraded and violated their bodies.

A defining feature of sexual abuse-related dissociation is the experience of body memories; nonverbal, somatic flashbacks in which the sensations of the abuse are relived in the body without corresponding cognitive recall. Children and later adults with DID may experience pain, pressure, or touch sensations that have no apparent cause, often triggered by subtle environmental cues. Body memories can be deeply distressing and contribute to feelings of confusion, shame, and lack of bodily ownership. Moreover, since sexual abuse often involves coercion, manipulation, or secrecy, victims may develop intense self-blame and internal conflict, further reinforcing the fragmentation of identity.

Sexual abuse also undermines the development of healthy attachment and emotional regulation. The child may struggle with intense feelings of fear, disgust, betrayal, and helplessness that are difficult to integrate. Over time, these unresolved emotions may become isolated within specific identity states, leading to emotional dysregulation, identity confusion, and persistent dissociative symptoms. The child may also experience memory gaps, a fluctuating sense of self, and internal voices or dialogues between identity states.

Childhood sexual abuse is one of the most potent precursors to dissociative identity disorder. The overwhelming, confusing, and often prolonged nature of the trauma, especially when inflicted by trusted caregivers, forces the child into a dissociative process that disrupts the linear nature of the developing self. Although splitting into different parts or identities helps the child survive extreme trauma, it often causes serious problems later in life, such as mood swings, trouble knowing who they are, and deep inner struggles. Understanding how sexual abuse can lead to this kind of condition is very important for giving the right kind of support and therapy to those affected.

Ritual abuse

Ritual abuse in children is a particularly severe and insidious form of trauma that involves repeated, systematic acts of physical, sexual, psychological, and emotional abuse, often within a cult-like or organized context. These acts are typically carried out by multiple perpetrators and are designed to exert total control over the child's mind, body, and behavior. Ritual abuse often incorporates elements of ideology, whether religious, pseudo-spiritual, or occult, and uses rituals, symbols, and repeated conditioning to instill fear, compliance, and psychological fragmentation. Though once dismissed or viewed as rare or sensationalized, growing clinical evidence and survivor testimony suggest that ritual abuse may be more widespread and pervasive than previously acknowledged, particularly among individuals with complex dissociative disorders such as dissociative identity disorder.

One of the most devastating aspects of ritual abuse is its deliberate and calculated use of psychological terror to break down a child's sense of self. Children subjected to such abuse are often forced to participate in or witness acts of extreme violence, degradation, or symbolic enactments meant to confuse moral reasoning and obliterate the boundaries between right and wrong. Perpetrators often employ techniques such as forced betrayals, the use of masks or costumes, sensory deprivation, mind-altering substances, and threats of death or harm to the child or their loved ones. These tactics are not random; they are intentionally designed to induce dissociation. The overwhelming and inescapable nature of the trauma, especially when combined with ritualistic repetition, causes the child's psyche to fragment in order to survive.

In the context of DID, ritual abuse is particularly significant because of its structural and repetitive nature. Unlike isolated incidents of abuse, ritual abuse often occurs over extended periods, with recurring episodes of terror and control. This ongoing exposure to trauma during early developmental stages severely impairs the formation of a single identity. In response, the child's mind creates dissociated self-states to compartmentalize the abuse. One identity might endure pain, another might hold secrets, and a third might manage daily life and appear functional to outsiders. Over time, these states become increasingly autonomous and differentiated, laying the groundwork for full-blown dissociative identity disorder.

Ritual abuse also instills layers of internal programming,

belief systems, self-blame, and directives designed to prevent disclosure or recovery. Survivors often report that parts of their psyche were conditioned to protect the abusers or deny the abuse entirely. This deep psychological conditioning can create formidable barriers to memory retrieval and healing, reinforcing dissociative amnesia and internal conflict between identity states. Furthermore, the use of symbolic and ritual elements during abuse confuses the child's sense of reality, blurring the line between real and imagined experiences, which complicates diagnosis and treatment in adulthood.

Clinicians and researchers are increasingly recognizing that individuals with DID often present with histories suggestive of ritual abuse, even when the survivor has difficulty articulating or consciously remembering the events. The highly organized and secretive nature of ritual abuse networks, combined with societal denial and limited forensic evidence, has contributed to the underreporting and misunderstanding of this form of trauma. Yet, the psychological profiles of many DID patients, particularly those with extensive dissociation, complex internal systems, and deep-seated fears of disclosure, reflect the patterns of conditioning consistent with ritual abuse histories. Acknowledging the existence and impact of ritual abuse is essential for validating survivor experiences and providing the specialized, trauma-informed care necessary for recovery and integration.

If there was any doubt of ritual abuse, at the time of writing this book, a case has come to light. At least seven adults, with a possible connection to an international human trafficking ring, have been arrested for raping, sodomizing, beating, using electrical devices, kidnapping, and using bondage on more than a dozen children; some as young as 2 years old. Ritual abuse is not new, yet when it comes to light, many do not recognize its connection with dissociative disorders. More than that, because ritual abuse is so heinous, many people refuse to acknowledge its existence, even when it is so very obvious. The average person cannot wrap their head around how evil other humans can be, and for this reason, too many children have been dismissed as making things up or being too imaginative.

Iatrogenic or fantasy model

The iatrogenic or fantasy model of DID asserts that the condition is not a naturally occurring psychological response to trauma, but rather an artifact produced by suggestive therapeutic techniques, cultural influence, and the power of imagination. According to proponents of this model, DID arises when therapists inadvertently implant false beliefs in susceptible individuals, often through hypnosis, guided imagery, or leading questions, causing them to believe they possess multiple identities. This theory suggests that individuals may unconsciously adopt the role of someone with DID, especially if they are highly imaginative, prone to fantasy, or seeking attention, thereby fabricating a condition that is ultimately shaped by the therapeutic relationship and media portrayals.

However, the iatrogenic model is widely regarded as a weak and insufficient explanation for DID, particularly when contrasted with the substantial empirical and clinical evidence supporting the trauma model. Critics of the iatrogenic viewpoint argue for the consistency and complexity of dissociative symptoms observed in patients across cultures, time periods, and therapeutic contexts, even in the absence of suggestive therapeutic practices. Many individuals with DID report amnesia, identity confusion, and internal conflict long before ever seeking treatment, undermining the claim that these symptoms are the result of therapeutic influence. Furthermore, DID is often underdiagnosed or misdiagnosed for years, which contradicts the notion that therapists are overzealously creating the disorder in their clients.

Scientific studies have further challenged the fantasy model by demonstrating that individuals with DID show measurable differences in brain activity, memory processing, and physiological responses across identity states. Neuroimaging research reveals distinct neural patterns between dissociative identity states, patterns that actors or individuals cannot voluntarily mimic without DID. Survivors frequently present with documented histories of severe and chronic trauma, particularly in early childhood, which aligns with the trauma model's assertion that DID is a defensive adaptation to overwhelming, inescapable abuse.

A complication to the diagnosis and believability of those who disclose sexual abuse and ritual abuse was the emergence of the False Memory Foundation, which emerged in the 1990s to challenge the validity of recovered memories of childhood sexual abuse, claiming that such memories were often the result of therapist suggestion and thus unreliable or entirely fabricated. However, this position has been widely criticized for misrepresenting the nature of traumatic memory and for minimizing the prevalence and impact of sexual abuse, particularly in relation to dissociative disorders. Empirical research demonstrates that traumatic memories, especially those involving early, repeated abuse can be dissociated and later recalled in fragmented or delayed ways, not due to suggestion, but because the mind protects itself from overwhelming pain. By promoting the notion that many survivors' memories are false, the False Memory Foundation has contributed to a harmful cultural skepticism that dismisses authentic trauma, silences survivors, and impedes accurate diagnosis and treatment of DID, which is often rooted in verified histories of prolonged sexual abuse. The validity of the foundation failed when it was revealed that those who began the foundation and those who were part of its board were accused pedophiles. The foundation is no longer in existence; however, its harmful rhetoric persists.

While the iatrogenic or fantasy model offers an alternative framework for understanding DID, it lacks empirical support and fails to account for the extensive clinical, neurological, and developmental evidence that aligns with the trauma-based origins of the disorder. Its reliance on assumptions about therapeutic suggestion and fantasy-proneness has contributed to harmful skepticism and stigmatization of survivors. The trauma model, grounded in decades of research and clinical observation, remains the most robust and ethically sound explanation for the development of DID. It's time to fully call the fantasy model what it is: utter shit!

Attachment as a Predictor

Attachment theory, developed by John Bowlby and later expanded by Mary Ainsworth and others, identifies four primary patterns of attachment that emerge in early childhood based on the child's relationship with primary caregivers: secure, anxious (ambivalent), avoidant, and disorganized. These attachment styles profoundly shape how individuals perceive themselves and others, regulate their emotions, and form relationships throughout their lives. For children exposed to abuse, neglect, or inconsistent caregiving, particularly during critical developmental stages, attachment disruptions can lead to profound psychological consequences. Of all attachment styles, disorganized attachment has the strongest and most direct correlation with the development of dissociative identity disorder.

Secure attachment arises when a caregiver is consistently responsive, attuned, and emotionally available. This allows the child to develop a stable sense of safety and trust, fostering self-confidence, emotional regulation, and healthy relationships. The child learns that distress will be met with comfort and that they are worthy of love and care. Individuals who are securely attached, approximately 50% of the population, tend to handle stress more effectively and form balanced interpersonal connections throughout their lives.

Anxious (ambivalent) attachment develops when caregiving is inconsistent, sometimes nurturing, other times neglectful. These children become hypervigilant and preoccupied with gaining approval and reassurance, fearing abandonment and doubting their worth. As adults, they may display dependency, emotional instability, and intense relational anxiety, always seeking closeness but fearing rejection. Individuals with this type of attachment represent approximately 15-20% of the population.

Avoidant attachment results when caregivers are emotionally distant, rejecting, or unresponsive. Children in this environment learn to suppress their emotional needs and avoid seeking comfort, believing their distress will be ignored. They often develop a façade of self-reliance and emotional detachment, which can carry into adulthood as difficulty with intimacy, empathy, or emotional expression. Individuals with this type of attachment represent approximately 15-20% of the population.

Disorganized attachment occurs when the caregiver is simultaneously a source of comfort and fear, typically due to abuse, neglect, or frightening, unpredictable behavior. This creates an unresolvable paradox for the child: the person they rely on for survival is also the source of terror. As a result, the child's internal attachment system becomes disoriented and fragmented. Without a coherent strategy for seeking safety or soothing, the child may enter a state of dissociative confusion, alternating between fear, withdrawal, hyperarousal, and emotional numbness. Internal chaos lays the groundwork for the development of dissociative mechanisms.

In individuals with DID, insecure attachment may be present but it is disorganized attachment most often evident in their deep ambivalence toward relationships, fluctuating trust in others, and inconsistent self-concept. Many experience internalized relational patterns where some identity states seek closeness while others fear or resist it. The profound disorientation and emotional fragmentation characteristic of disorganized attachment mirror the structural dissociation seen in DID, making this attachment style the most closely aligned with the disorder's developmental origins. Addressing and repairing disorganized attachment in therapy is therefore central to helping individuals with DID build internal coherence, develop emotional safety, and begin the process of relational healing.

Chapter 6 – Neurobiology

Neuronal Mechanism

Dissociative identity disorder represents a complex and often debated diagnosis within the psychiatric field, with ongoing research focusing on its neurobiological foundations to substantiate its legitimacy and enhance diagnostic precision. The existing body of research provides both the challenges and advancements in understanding the disorder. While some argue that structural irregularities in the brain alone cannot fully account for the diverse symptoms of DID, nor adequately resolve inconsistencies across findings, the growing body of brain anatomy evidence provides compelling support for its authenticity. However, these investigations face inherent difficulties, including limited sample sizes and a reliance on case studies, which do not comprehensively represent the affected population.

Despite hurdles, emerging studies have begun to uncover significant neurobiological distinctions between individuals with DID and healthy control groups. For instance, variations in white matter structure have been identified, offering a potential biomarker for DID. The growing repository of neurobiological data not only reinforces a valid diagnostic category but also aims to refine and enhance the reliability of existing diagnostic methodologies.

Neurobiological Structures and Alterations

The academic discussion surrounding dissociative identity disorder encompasses a broad spectrum of topics, including its etiology, symptomatic expressions, and the complexities inherent in its diagnosis. A significant body of research emphasizes the robust connection between DID and experiences of childhood trauma, proposing that dissociation emerges as a psychological mechanism aimed at mitigating the effects of overwhelming and often inescapable adversity. However, DID's validity as a psychiatric diagnosis has not been without contention. Contrasting viewpoints within the medical community have sparked debates, with some critics refuting DID as a "medical fad." In response, advocates for DID's recognition underline the necessity of accurate diagnostic practices and the implementation of compassionate treatment frameworks. Further exploration delves into the disorder's neurobiological dimensions, presenting evidence on brain structure and activity, particularly in relation to memory impairments and dissociative phenomena. While there is a growing body of evidence supporting a tangible neurobiological basis for DID, the field remains in developmental stages.

Key Brain Regions and Structural Alterations

Hippocampus

Research has identified significant alterations in the hippocampus among patients diagnosed with dissociative identity disorder and post-traumatic stress disorder (PTSD). Both hippocampi tend to be smaller in DID and PTSD patients when compared to healthy controls. People with DID tend to have a smaller left side of the hippocampus, a part of the brain important for memory integration and recall, compared to people with PTSD. There's also a pattern of the right side of the hippocampus being smaller, though this is less pronounced. The reduced hippocampal volume is particularly significant in understanding DID-related symptoms such as memory impairment and dissociative amnesia.

The decade of the brain (1990s) has provided us with the means to examine, confirm, and refute previous theories on DID. Emerging studies suggest that hippocampal volume may exhibit potential for recovery following targeted interventions, including medication or phase-oriented psychotherapy. The need for therapeutic strategies aimed at addressing the neurobiological consequences of trauma in DID patients is paramount.

DID patients often exhibit significantly smaller hippocampal volumes compared to healthy controls, with one study reporting a 19.2% reduction in female DID patients. Specific subfields, such as bilateral CA1, right CA4, and right granule cell molecular layer of the dentate gyrus, show notable reductions. These findings suggest a strong correlation between hippocampal alterations and memory impairments, particularly dissociative amnesia, as CA1 volume reductions uniquely link to this symptom.

Research also shows that the more severe a person's early experiences of trauma or neglect, the smaller their hippocampus tends to be. However, there's some good news: people with DID who begin to recover often have larger hippocampi than those who don't, suggesting that the brain can heal and even regrow some of its structures over time.

Amygdala

The amygdala has been the subject of extensive research regarding its role in dissociative identity disorder, yet findings remain inconclusive. While some studies highlight a reduction in amygdalar volume among DID patients compared to healthy controls, others fail to identify significant differences when comparing DID individuals to those diagnosed with PTSD. This discrepancy is partly attributable to the limited availability of meta-analytic data and the varying methodologies employed across studies.

One meta-analysis, referenced in a review by Blihar et al. (2020), points to notable changes in the left amygdala-hippocampal junction and a potential loss of amygdala volume as critical neuroanatomical features underlying DID. The alterations are particularly relevant to depersonalization, a hallmark symptom of the disorder. The reduced size and function of the amygdala are hypothesized to play a pivotal role in the manifestation of DID, possibly reflecting the brain's reliance on dissociative defense mechanisms to cope with overwhelming fear stimuli.

In simpler terms, brain scans show that the way certain parts of the brain "talk" to each other can be different in people with DID. For example, areas that help control emotions might not work together as well as they should. This can lead to the brain handling strong feelings in a less healthy way, which may play a role in the symptoms seen in DID. More studies are needed to gain a deeper understanding of the amygdala's role in dissociation and emotional processing.

Frontal Cortex

The frontal cortex has been identified as an area of interest in patients with dissociative identity disorder, with studies revealing reduced cortical and subcortical volumes in regions responsible for movement execution and fear learning. The frontal cortex is best known for its role in executive functioning, higher-level learning, decision-making, and impulse control. Of particular significance are the orbitofrontal cortex (OFC), located on the underside of the prefrontal cortex and responsible for social relationships, emotional regulation, and decision-making, and the anterior cingulate cortex (ACC), located deeper within the prefrontal cortex and wrapped around the corpus callosum (the communication center of the brain) and responsible for critical thinking, emotional regulation, and decision-making. Both the OFC and ACC exhibit decreased size and activity in individuals with DID. When this part of the brain is smaller, people might not react to fear the same way others do; responses are blunted and do not appear to activate the survival system in the same way. Similarly, having smaller areas that help manage emotions and motivation can make it harder for someone to handle feelings of fear or stay motivated.

A decrease in cortical thickness (grey matter that covers the outer portion of the brain) in the left frontal cortex, along with smaller dimensions of various frontal regions, including Broca's area and deep cingulate regions, lends further support to the hypothesis that trauma exerts a detrimental influence on frontal cortical structures. Functional imaging studies have also highlighted the inhibition of frontal cortex activity, along with temporal and hippocampal regions, during episodes of dissociative amnesia.

In the left region of the frontal cortex (though close to the left temporal lobe) is a region associated with language perception and production, the Broca's area. Studies have indicated that when overwhelming events occur, the Broca's area becomes nearly inactive, making it almost impossible to speak, write, or express what the person is thinking or feeling. This is a phenomenon called aphasia. Trauma model theories suggest that this breaking down of language production leaves victims of trauma and extreme events without the ability to tell their story. In people with DID, this pervasive shut-down means their story remains, not just inaccessible, but unable to be told. Whether the event occurred days prior to interacting with a helping professional or trusted adult, or years later, the initial shut-down of language production remains intact and related to the specific trauma from which it first occurred. Therapeutically, this means that getting individuals to disclose and process their memories may require some creative thinking.

Parietal Region

Parietal structures in patients with DID have revealed significant reductions in both cortical and subcortical volumes, particularly in regions associated with sensory perception and self-awareness. The parietal region of the brain is located just behind the frontal cortex, approximately at the center-top of the brain. A diminished inferior parietal cortex (located deeper within the parietal region and responsible for receiving and processing sensory information and special awareness) has been linked to the expression and interpretation challenges often observed in individuals with DID, as well as to episodes of derealization reported in different parts.

Abnormalities in the angular gyrus and supramarginal gyrus (located within the inferior parietal region) have been identified, with reduced sizes in these regions correlating with difficulties in self-awareness and expressive capacities (language development). The postcentral gyrus, which encompasses the primary somatosensory cortex (S1), has demonstrated a notable role in tasks requiring a first-person perspective. Interestingly, a larger postcentral gyrus has been associated with heightened dissociative states, suggesting its potential contribution to the altered sensory and perceptual experiences commonly seen in DID patients.

Insula

Research has identified significant alterations in the insular cortex, located deep within the lateral sulcus (the fissure between the frontal cortex and the parietal cortex), which is responsible for processing sensory information, including pain, motor function, and social interpretation, in patients diagnosed with DID. Specifically, a reduction in the volume of the insula has been consistently noted.

This diminished structure is hypothesized to contribute to an increased susceptibility to phenomena such as hallucinations and episodes of derealization, particularly during traumatic events.

The insular cortex, recognized for its role in self-awareness and emotional processing, appears to play a critical part in the disconnection from reality reported by many DID patients. A notable reduction in insular activation has been observed among individuals experiencing dissociative amnesia during memory recognition tasks. The decreased activity suggests a potential link between insular dysfunction and the impaired ability to access or process memories.

Basal Ganglia

Studies of the basal ganglia in patients diagnosed with DID have revealed noteworthy differences in structure and function compared to healthy controls and individuals with other trauma-related conditions. The basal ganglia are a network of connections that are located deep within the center of the brain and are responsible for memory, learning, integration, sensory perception, motor control, motivation, reward, and decision-making. Specifically, the putamen and pallidum have exhibited significantly larger volumes, a finding corroborated by fMRI studies showing increased activity in the putamen when DID patients observed facial expressions while in a dissociated state. These structural and functional anomalies suggest a potential link between basal ganglia alterations and the distinct movement patterns or habits observed across different personalities in DID.

Additionally, research has identified lower fractional anisotropy (FA), indicative of reduced white matter integrity, in the bilateral pallidum of DID patients in comparison to healthy individuals, and in the left pallidum when compared to PTSD patients. This reduction in FA has been further correlated with higher levels of depersonalization as well as childhood emotional neglect and abuse. The role of deep brain structures like the basal ganglia in regulating movement highlights their possible involvement in the unique psychobiological characteristics of DID. New insights continue to advance the understanding of how early trauma may manifest in alterations in brain connectivity and function, contributing to the complex presentation of dissociative phenomena.

Other brain structures

Studies of additional brain structures in DID patients have revealed significant variations that may contribute to the disorder's complex presentation. White matter tracts, which facilitate communication between somatosensory association areas, the basal ganglia, and the precuneus, were notably larger in DID individuals. Specifically, increased white matter was identified in motor regions within the brainstem and the right hemisphere. These findings may explain the distinct mannerisms, differences in handedness, and varying physical skill levels observed across different identity states.

The parahippocampal and fusiform gyri, located in the temporal and occipital lobes, also demonstrate alterations in DID patients, with these regions being closely linked to symptoms of intrusive thoughts and difficulties with recall. Research indicates a marked over-activation of the parahippocampal gyri during emotionally dissociated states, contrasting with under-activation in neutral states.

Other regions impacted by DID include the occipital cortex, which has been found to be smaller in patients with the disorder, and the cingulate cortex, which plays a critical role in emotional regulation and cognitive processes. These findings collectively enrich our understanding of the neurobiological underpinnings of DID, highlighting the intricate interplay between structural and functional cerebral changes that characterize this complex condition.

Functional Alterations and Identity States

Functional neuroimaging techniques, such as functional MRI and PET scans, have identified significant alterations in neural activity in individuals diagnosed with dissociative identity disorder (DID). Specifically, these studies reveal reduced activity in the right inferior lateral prefrontal cortex, which is believed to play a role in the regulation of identity states and emotional responses (apparent normal parts (ANPs) and emotional parts (EPs), or neutral identity states (NIS) and traumatic identity states (TIS)).

Research has documented notable psychobiological differences between neutral identity states and traumatic identity states, particularly in response to trauma-related scripts. For instance, distinct patterns of subjective emotional ratings, heart rate, and regional cerebral blood flow have been observed when individuals transition between NIS and TIS. Each state exhibits unique neural and physiological reactivity to trauma-related and other psychological stimuli.

One study demonstrated that individuals in a traumatic identity state exhibited elevated heart rate and blood pressure when exposed to a trauma-related script, a response that was absent when the same individuals were in their neutral identity state. These findings contribute to the growing body of research that highlights the complex interaction between psychobiological mechanisms and dissociative phenomena.

Genetic and Epigenetic Factors

Genetic and epigenetic factors are increasingly recognized as significant contributors to the development of DID. Although research in this area remains in its early stages, evidence suggests that the capacity for dissociation may have a heritable component.

Studies have identified specific genetic polymorphisms that could influence susceptibility to DID. These include genes associated with monoaminergic transmission, such as 5-HTTLPR and COMT, as well as those involved in neuroplasticity, including BDNF, and the regulation of the stress response, such as FKBP5.

The role of FKBP5 (a protein within genes) has garnered attention due to its interaction with early-life trauma. Variations in FKBP5 haplotypes (groups of polymorphisms) appear to increase the likelihood of dissociative tendencies when combined with adverse childhood experiences. These findings emphasize the importance of considering both genetic predispositions and environmental triggers in understanding the development of DID. By integrating neurobiological, genetic, and epigenetic perspectives, researchers are making strides toward a more comprehensive understanding of the complex mechanisms underlying this disorder.

Relationship with Trauma

An intrinsic connection exists between dissociative identity disorder and trauma, with the majority of DID patients recounting experiences of severe childhood adversity. These experiences often encompass a spectrum of abuse and neglect, including physical and emotional maltreatment, as well as sexual abuse. The disorder is widely understood as a posttraumatic developmental condition that originates in childhood. Prolonged exposure to a hostile and aversive environment during formative years forces the brain to compartmentalize cognitive and emotional states along with memories, thereby facilitating the emergence of dissociative self-states.

Incorporating neurobiological studies in the topic of dissociative disorders and early childhood trauma has led us to understand that there is so much more to learn. However, what has been discovered through neurobiological studies indicates that those with DID exhibit differences when switches between personality states occur, language processing and development is profoundly impacted, personality states impact motor control and mannerisms, the survival system can be overactive or blunted, emotional processing impacts social relationships, critical thinking and impulse control is diminished, and memory integration and recall are incredibly fragmented.

Comparison to Other Disorders
The comparison of DID to other psychological disorders highlights key distinctions and overlaps in symptomology and neurobiological characteristics. Patients diagnosed with DID often exhibit more severe dissociative symptoms compared to those with post-traumatic stress disorder (PTSD). People with DID often have smaller overall brain sizes, but this isn't unique to them. Similar decreases in brain size are also seen in other mental health conditions like PTSD, borderline personality disorder, and dissociative amnesia. Because of this, having a smaller brain volume alone can't be used to clearly identify someone as having DID.

Despite the high comorbidity between DID and PTSD, efforts are ongoing to differentiate the unique neurobiological signatures of DID. One distinguishing feature is the presence of dissociative self-states in DID, which is not commonly observed in disorders like PTSD or BPD. Distinct patterns of brain activation further set DID apart. For instance, while alterations in the size of the amygdala and hippocampus are often associated with PTSD symptomatology, emerging research suggests that reduced hippocampal volumes in DID may extend beyond those observed in PTSD.

Neuroimaging studies have revealed that individuals with DID and dissociative PTSD display more overlapping patterns of brain activation compared to those with depersonalization/derealization disorder (DPD). DPD patients, in particular, often exhibit diverging structural and functional brain patterns, indicating that the underlying mechanisms of their symptoms may differ significantly from those of DID. These findings call attention to the complexity of neurobiological distinctions among dissociative disorders and emphasize the need for further research to refine diagnostic approaches and therapeutic interventions. The connection between DID and PTSD is this; you can have PTSD without DID, but you cannot have DID without also having PTSD.

Limitations and Future Directions

The field of neurobiological research in dissociative identity disorder is still in its formative stages, with several limitations that must be addressed. Notably, there is a pressing need for studies with larger sample sizes that can yield more statistically robust findings. Future research would benefit from controlling for a broader range of variables to ensure the specificity and accuracy of observed results. For instance, including control groups of PTSD patients without dissociative symptoms or accounting for the severity of PTSD symptoms as a covariate could help delineate the neurobiological alterations that are unique to DID.

An important area for further investigation is the determination of whether the neurobiological abnormalities observed in DID were there prior to the onset of symptoms or if they develop because of prolonged dissociative processing. Longitudinal studies, combined with advanced quantitative analyses, are crucial for addressing this question. Such research could also illuminate the trajectory of neurobiological changes over time and their relationship to symptom progression.

To better help people with DID, experts are working to find new treatments that address the specific changes seen in the brains of those with the disorder. Because DID is complicated and often happens alongside other mental health issues, understanding brain scans and medical results can be tricky. That is why researchers are working hard to develop more accurate ways to diagnose and treat DID, based on its unique brain features, ensuring that the help people receive is tailored to their specific needs.

Neurobiological research into DID is progressing toward establishing a well-defined neuroanatomical basis for the condition. This effort represents a significant step in addressing long-standing controversies surrounding the disorder. Emerging findings consistently demonstrate structural and functional alterations in several critical brain regions, including the hippocampus, amygdala, and various cortical and subcortical areas. These regions are intimately involved in processes related to memory, emotional regulation, and the construction of self-identity.

Chapter 7 - Common Comorbidities

The prevalence of DID in the general population is estimated to range between 1% and 1.5%, a rate comparable to that of schizophrenia, demonstrating its significant presence despite frequent underrecognition and misdiagnosis. DID is rarely encountered as a standalone diagnosis; it is typically accompanied by a diverse array of psychiatric and physical comorbidities, further complicating its identification and management. It is important that researchers, clinicians, and even those with DID take a nuanced approach to understanding the disorder within broader psychiatric frameworks.

Post Traumatic Stress Disorder (PTSD)
Post-traumatic stress disorder (PTSD) frequently co-occurs with dissociative identity disorder, with many experts considering DID to represent the most severe manifestation of childhood-onset PTSD. Both conditions share numerous features, particularly their origins in trauma; however, DID is distinguished by the additional hallmark of identity disruption. Studies indicate that between 80% and 100% of individuals diagnosed with DID also meet the diagnostic criteria for PTSD, highlighting the deep

interconnectedness of these disorders. The connection between DID and PTSD is this: you can have PTSD without DID, but you likely will not have DID without also having PTSD.

A defining feature that differentiates DID from PTSD lies in the severity of dissociative experiences, particularly the amnesia occurring between identity states. This disruption, experienced by the "host" identity and alternate identities, serves as a critical marker of DID, setting it apart as a distinct yet related condition within the broader trauma spectrum.

Mood Disorders
Mood disorders, particularly major depressive disorder (MDD), are pervasive among individuals diagnosed with dissociative identity disorder (DID). Studies indicate that nearly all DID patients, 98.1% in one specific study, experience some form of mood disorder, with 97.2% reporting major depressive episodes. This high rate shows just how much childhood trauma can affect people, since it is commonly found in both DID and depression.

Researchers have found that people with DID who also struggle with mood disorders like depression often show severe dissociation and anxious attachment styles as adults. This means that unresolved trauma can show up as both identity issues and persistent feelings of sadness, hopelessness, or anxiety. Recognizing how these experiences overlap helps therapists design treatments that tackle both dissociative and depressive symptoms together.

Personality Disorders
Personality disorders, particularly borderline personality disorder (BPD), are frequently observed in patients with dissociative identity disorder. More than half of people with DID, about 56.3% according to one study, also have BPD. Just like PTSD and DID, this big overlap

between DID and BPD shows just how much these two conditions have in common, especially since both are closely linked to childhood trauma.

Borderline personality disorder is characterized by a range of symptoms that include unstable interpersonal relationships, unpredictable mood fluctuations, impulsive behaviors, an extreme fear of abandonment, and self-injurious actions. These features are often conceptualized as trauma-related, which aligns with the dissociative experiences observed in DID. Individuals diagnosed with BPD frequently report a history of significant childhood adversities, suggesting shared etiological factors with DID.

While the clinical manifestations of DID and BPD may sometimes appear similar, including the presence of emotional instability and trauma-related symptoms, they represent distinct diagnostic entities. Some experts propose that the two disorders may be variations on a continuum of trauma-related psychopathology, emphasizing the importance of nuanced clinical assessment to differentiate them and tailor treatment approaches effectively.

Psychotic Disorders

Psychotic disorders, particularly those within the schizophrenia spectrum, are often associated with symptoms that can overlap with the clinical presentation of DID. These include auditory hallucinations and delusional beliefs, which may lead to diagnostic confusion. Research indicates that a significant proportion of individuals diagnosed with DID, 74.3% in one study, carry a concurrent diagnosis of some form of psychotic disorder, such as schizoaffective disorder (49.5%) or schizophrenia (18.7%). Despite these overlaps, the hallucinatory experiences reported by DID patients are typically distinct from those observed in psychotic disorders. For instance, auditory hallucinations in DID often stem from alter personalities within the individual's psyche and are known to resolve following therapeutic integration of these alters. The differentiation between DID and psychotic disorders is critical for ensuring accurate diagnosis and effective treatment plans. Using solid diagnostic tools and understanding exactly where symptoms come from helps doctors tell these conditions apart. This way, they can avoid misdiagnoses and make sure people get treatment that really fits their needs. For instance, as a clinician, if you diagnose an individual with schizophrenia based solely on auditory, visual, or sensorimotor hallucinations, you may miss the more poignant diagnosis. If a client with DID is misdiagnosed with schizophrenia, the interventions are often quite different, making the differentiation critical for your client.

Dissociative Amnesia (DA) and Dissociative Fugue (DF)

Dissociative amnesia is a primary feature of dissociative identity disorder (DID) and is often observed in conjunction with the condition. Many individuals with DID exhibit extensive amnesia concerning personal information, which significantly impacts their daily lives and their ability to recall key aspects of their identities.

Closely associated with dissociative amnesia is dissociative fugue, a phenomenon previously categorized as a subtype of dissociative amnesia in the DSM-5. This condition involves sudden, unexpected travel away from an individual's usual surroundings, accompanied by an inability to recall one's past or identity. Patients with dissociative amnesia frequently present other accompanying dissociative symptoms, including depersonalization, spontaneous trance states, and age regression, further complicating their clinical presentations. Even though DA and DF are common symptoms of those with DID, it does not automatically mean that those experiencing amnesia or fugue states have DID. Remember, DID's prime characteristic is the presence of two or more personality states; accompanying symptoms are auxiliary.

Anxiety disorders and dissociative disorders (DDs)

Anxiety disorders are frequently observed as comorbid conditions in individuals with dissociative disorders (DDs), including dissociative identity disorder, presenting substantial complexity in both diagnosis and treatment due to their prevalence and overlapping symptomatology. Research has revealed high rates of comorbidity between anxiety disorders. Frequently observed conditions include panic disorder, obsessive-compulsive disorder (OCD), and social phobia. Intermediate prevalence rates have been noted for specific phobia and agoraphobia, while generalized anxiety disorder appears less common, with rates comparable to those in the general population. Epidemiological studies have highlighted the frequent coexistence of dissociative disorders with depressive disorders (51.42%) and anxiety disorders (50%).

The relationship between anxiety disorders and trauma complicates the clinical picture. Trauma, particularly childhood maltreatment, is strongly associated with the development of anxiety disorders and other psychiatric conditions. Epidemiological studies have established links between childhood sexual abuse and various psychiatric disorders, including anxiety disorders and dissociation.

When we talk about "dissociation," we're really describing a wide range of experiences. It can mean anything from normal moments when your mind wanders to deeper reactions that people develop after trauma, like mental defenses or changes in how the brain handles stress. Because dissociation covers so much ground, it can be tricky for clinicians to pin down exactly what's going on, so it's important to take a careful and practical approach to diagnosis and treatment. In short, anxiety disorders and dissociation often go hand in hand, usually because they share roots in past trauma. Since their symptoms overlap and they show up together so often, clinicians have to make sure they look closely at each case to figure out the best way to help.

Eating disorders and DID

People with dissociative identity disorder (DID) often also struggle with eating disorders, and these issues usually trace back to tough childhood experiences and dissociation. Studies show that eating disorders show up frequently in folks with DID, especially when dissociative episodes trigger binge-eating.

Data shows that people who went through sexual abuse as children are much more likely to develop eating disorders, and the severity of trauma plays a big role in how serious binge-eating symptoms can be. Problems with managing emotions often link trauma to eating difficulties. All of these points point to the complicated nature of treating these overlapping conditions and show why a trauma-informed approach is key.

Interestingly, some patients with DID who were treated in eating disorder units reported feeling out of place, suggesting that their dissociative symptoms were not adequately recognized or addressed within such settings. This highlights the importance of a nuanced and comprehensive understanding of DID when evaluating and treating patients with complex comorbidities.

Substance Use Disorder and DID

Substance use disorder (SUD) has been identified as a significant comorbidity in individuals with dissociative disorders. This association is often observed within the broader context of childhood trauma, which is a common foundation for both dissociative disorders and substance abuse. Research highlights the prevalence and severity of substance abuse among DID patients, with many reporting alcohol and drug addiction as concurrent diagnoses. Some people start using substances as early as childhood or their teen years, which really shows how much early trauma can affect them later on. There are even cases where someone suddenly stops heavy substance use on their own, without going through any official treatment. This just goes to show how unique these experiences can be.

Childhood trauma, particularly sexual abuse, has been strongly linked to substance abuse. Studies suggest a dose-response relationship between the severity and duration of early maltreatment and the likelihood of developing addiction issues. Forms of childhood adversity, such as abuse, neglect, and household dysfunction, have been associated with an increased risk of illicit drug use. Betrayal trauma, a specific type of childhood trauma, has been connected to substance use as well as dissociative post-traumatic stress symptoms. Chronic depersonalization, a dissociative symptom, has reportedly emerged during episodes of substance abuse, offering insight into the interplay between dissociation and addiction.

The comorbidity of substance abuse and dissociative disorders presents distinct diagnostic challenges. Symptoms attributable to substance use must be carefully distinguished from those of dissociative disorders to ensure accurate diagnosis and treatment. The presence of substance abuse alongside other conditions such as PTSD, panic disorder, phobias, and major depression complicates this process further. Studies propose that dissociation, PTSD, and substance use may share direct and mediated pathways, emphasizing the need for integrated approaches in diagnosis and intervention. A harm reduction framework tailored to individuals with co-occurring opioid use disorder (OUD) and trauma-related conditions has been recommended for effective treatment.

Conversion Disorder and DID

Conversion Disorder (CD), also known as Functional Neurological Symptom Disorder in the DSM-5, has been discussed in diagnostic literature for its classification and association with other disorders. Historically, the term "conversion" has been utilized, particularly within the ICD-10, to describe conditions where unresolved emotional conflicts manifest as physical symptoms. In earlier iterations of the DSM, Conversion Disorder was grouped under somatoform disorders, though recommendations have been made to realign it with dissociative disorders (DDs) in the DSM-5. This proposed reclassification stems from the idea that dissociation, as a psychological mechanism, can serve as an adaptive response to acute or chronic trauma, aiding survival in situations of inescapable threat. Historically, the DSM-II distinguished "Hysterical Neurosis" into "Conversion type" and "Dissociative type," illuminating the connection between these classifications.

Conversion Disorder is primarily characterized by somatic symptoms (physical symptoms with no medical explanation) that are qualitatively distinct from those typically assessed in conditions such as PTSD, borderline personality disorder (BPD), and other dissociative disorders. The neurobiological underpinnings of Conversion Disorder are thought to involve mechanisms distinct from those associated with other forms of dissociation. Despite these differences, research findings indicate that somatoform symptoms can co-occur with dissociative symptoms across various levels of severity. Interestingly, this co-occurrence appears to be independent of the overall severity of dissociation or the prevalence of childhood maltreatment. Emerging evidence also suggests that emotional maltreatment, particularly within the context of dysfunctional family dynamics, may contribute to the development of somatoform symptoms.

The relationship between Conversion Disorder and dissociation is further highlighted by reports of somatic symptoms associated with dissociative episodes. For instance, nightmare disorders and nocturnal dissociative episodes have been documented as manifestations of dissociative disorders. These phenomena often involve a blending of conscious states, including the voluntary alteration of dreams and other mindful activities, which may indicate predispositions toward both dissociative and conversion experiences.

The high degree of comorbidity between dissociative identity disorder and other psychiatric conditions such as PTSD, mood disorders, anxiety, substance abuse, and eating disorders, complicates the diagnostic process for Conversion Disorder. The ongoing debate about the classification of Conversion Disorder within the DSM framework reflects a broader discussion about the adaptive and maladaptive characteristics of dissociation.

The extensive comorbidity associated with DID complicates its diagnosis, making purely dissociative disorders exceedingly rare. DID is often accompanied by other mental health conditions, and patients may experience a variety of interconnected symptoms that reflect a broader response to chronic and severe childhood trauma. Researchers have posited that these various diagnoses could be elements of a larger "superordinate syndrome." Due to these complexities, DID patients commonly spend an average of 6.7 years within the mental health system before receiving an accurate diagnosis, highlighting the challenges in identifying and managing this multifaceted disorder.

Challenges in Diagnosis due to Comorbidity

The extensive comorbidity observed in individuals with DID presents substantial challenges to accurate diagnosis. The symptoms often overlap with or mimic those of various other psychiatric disorders, complicating the diagnostic process. A purely dissociative presentation is rare, as multiple comorbid conditions typically accompany DID. This prevalence of co-occurring disorders is a primary factor contributing to the difficulties clinicians face when attempting to establish an accurate diagnosis.

As a result, individuals with DID are frequently misdiagnosed or underdiagnosed, leading to treatment approaches that fail to address the underlying condition effectively. The diagnostic framework itself presents a paradox, wherein a formal diagnosis is often required to access specialized care. However, skepticism surrounding the validity of a DID diagnosis can impede access to appropriate treatment, further exacerbating the challenges faced by patients. This situation not only hinders effective intervention but also risks deepening the patient's sense of disconnection and fragmentation.

Chapter 8 - Non-clinical Therapeutic Practices

Healing from trauma, particularly childhood trauma, involves more than clinical interventions; it demands a holistic approach that addresses both the mind and body. Non-clinical therapeutic techniques offer invaluable tools to complement traditional psychotherapy by fostering emotional regulation, reconnecting individuals to their physical selves, and promoting resilience. From mindfulness practices and yoga to expressive therapies and grounding techniques, these approaches empower survivors to navigate their journey with self-compassion and agency. By integrating these practices into daily life, individuals can transform their pain into a pathway for growth and renewal. This section explores a variety of non-clinical methods, providing practical insights and strategies for trauma recovery and emotional well-being.

Yoga

Yoga is a holistic practice that integrates physical movement, breath regulation, and mindfulness to promote emotional and physical well-being. For individuals with a history of trauma, PTSD, or dissociative symptoms, yoga can serve as a grounding practice that reconnects them with their bodies, which may feel alien or unsafe due to the effects of trauma.

How to Practice: Begin with a simple flow sequence such as child's pose, cat-cow stretches, or seated breathing exercises. Focus on slow, deliberate movements and synchronize them with deep, rhythmic breathing. Trauma-sensitive yoga often emphasizes choice, inviting participants to adapt poses to their comfort level. Avoid poses that feel overly exposing or triggering and instead prioritize positions that promote a sense of security, such as reclining postures or poses close to the ground.

Why It Works: Trauma often disrupts the connection between the mind and body, leading to feelings of disembodiment or emotional dysregulation. Yoga helps to reestablish this connection by activating the parasympathetic nervous system, which calms the body's stress responses. The deliberate focus on breath and movement fosters mindfulness, reducing hypervigilance and promoting a sense of safety in the present moment.

Meditation

Meditation is a mental exercise aimed at cultivating awareness and fostering a sense of inner calm. For trauma survivors, guided or mindfulness-based meditation can serve as a tool to interrupt intrusive thoughts, regulate emotions, and build a sense of control over their inner experiences.

How to Practice: Find a quiet, comfortable place to sit or lie down. Close your eyes, and focus on your breath, allowing it to become slow and steady. Acknowledge any thoughts or feelings that arise without judgment and gently redirect your focus back to your breath. For beginners, guided meditations that use calming visualizations or phrases like "I am safe" can be particularly effective.

Why It Works: Meditation reduces the activity in the

amygdala, the brain region associated with fear and stress responses. By encouraging non-reactivity to thoughts and sensations, it helps trauma survivors gain greater control over their mental states. Over time, meditation can reduce the frequency and intensity of flashbacks or emotional overwhelm.

Mindfulness Practices

Mindfulness involves cultivating a focused awareness of the present moment, often through sensory engagement. It is particularly effective for individuals with PTSD or dissociative symptoms, as it helps anchor them to the here and now, counteracting feelings of detachment or hyperarousal.

How to Practice: Engage in grounding exercises such as the "5-4-3-2-1" technique. Identify 5 things you can see, 4 things you can touch, 3 things you can hear, 2 things you can smell, and 1 thing you can taste. Alternatively, practice mindful eating by concentrating on the texture, flavor, and aroma of each bite of food.

Why It Works: Mindfulness practices directly counteract dissociation, a common coping mechanism for trauma survivors. By focusing on sensory experiences, individuals can reconnect with their bodies and surroundings, fostering a sense of safety and presence. Regular mindfulness exercises also improve emotional regulation and reduce the likelihood of being overwhelmed by intrusive memories.

Expressive Therapies

Expressive therapies involve creative outlets, such as art, music, or writing, to explore and process emotions in a safe and nonverbal way. These practices offer trauma survivors an alternative medium to convey thoughts and feelings that may be difficult to articulate through traditional conversation.

How to Practice: Start with a medium that feels most

comfortable: drawing, journaling, or even playing a musical instrument. For example, create a piece of artwork that represents your emotions or write a letter to your past self as a means of self-compassion. The goal is not artistic perfection but rather emotional expression and exploration.

Why It Works: Trauma often resides in implicit, non-verbal memory, making it hard to address through cognitive processing alone. Expressive therapies bypass this barrier by engaging the right hemisphere of the brain, which is responsible for creativity and emotional expression. These activities provide a safe outlet for pent-up emotions, promote self-awareness, and facilitate emotional release.

Grounding Techniques

Grounding techniques are strategies designed to help individuals detach from overwhelming emotions or memories and refocus on the present. These are particularly helpful for those experiencing flashbacks, panic attacks, or dissociative episodes.

How to Practice: Use physical grounding strategies such as holding an ice cube, stomping your feet, or splashing cool water on your face. Verbal grounding techniques might include describing your surroundings in detail or repeating affirmations like "I am here, I am safe." Mental grounding exercises can include counting backward from 100 or naming items in a specific category.

Why It Works: Grounding techniques activate the prefrontal cortex, the logical part of the brain, which helps override emotional and fear-driven responses from the amygdala. By redirecting focus to the external environment, grounding reduces the intensity of traumatic memories and helps individuals maintain a sense of control during distressing episodes.

Physical Movement and Exercise

Physical movement, including dance, walking, or fitness routines, can be a powerful intervention for trauma recovery. It allows for the release of pent-up tension and helps individuals feel more in tune with their bodies.

How to Practice: Choose an activity that feels enjoyable and accessible, such as a brisk walk in nature, a light dance session to your favorite music, or even structured exercises like tai chi. The key is to focus on the sensations of movement and the rhythm of your breath.

Why It Works: Trauma often leads to stored tension and hyperactivation in the body. Physical movement helps release this energy, promoting relaxation and reducing symptoms of hyperarousal. Exercise also increases the production of endorphins, natural chemicals that improve mood and foster a sense of well-being.

Nature Exposure

Spending time in natural settings has been shown to reduce stress levels and enhance emotional resilience. For trauma survivors, nature exposure can provide a calming and restorative environment that facilitates healing.

How to Practice: Spend time in a local park, near a body of water, or in a forest. Engage your senses by feeling the texture of leaves, listening to the sounds of birds, or observing the changing light of the sky. Activities like gardening or hiking can also be deeply grounding.

Why It Works: Nature exposure lowers cortisol levels, the body's primary stress hormone, and promotes a sense of tranquility. The sensory richness of natural environments encourages mindfulness and helps individuals escape the mental loops of trauma-related thoughts.

Spiritual and ritual practices offer trauma survivors a deeply personal and meaningful way to engage with their healing journey. Personal rituals, such as lighting candles, writing letters to release emotions, or engaging in symbolic cleansing practices, serve as a form of emotional closure. These acts provide a structured way to process and let go of pain and negative feelings, creating a sense of renewal and hope.

Meditative prayer or contemplation can also play a significant role, especially for those who operate within spiritual or religious frameworks. By fostering a space of quiet reflection and connection to a higher purpose or meaning, these practices help individuals make sense of their experiences and transform their suffering into growth. This process of meaning-making not only alleviates emotional distress but also builds a foundation of inner peace and resilience.

Additionally, the use of affirmations and mantras contributes to the rebuilding of self-worth and the dismantling of internalized shame. By repeating intentional and positive self-talk, individuals can reshape negative thought patterns and foster a more compassionate relationship with themselves. This method works by rewiring neural pathways in the brain, gradually replacing feelings of inadequacy with empowerment and self-acceptance.

Incorporating spiritual and ritual practices into trauma recovery brings a sense of agency and connection to something greater than oneself. These techniques are not only deeply personal but also versatile, allowing individuals to adapt them to their unique needs and beliefs. Over time, they can foster a sense of stability and transformation, empowering survivors to navigate their healing journeys with renewed strength and purpose.

Self-Hypnosis and Parts Negotiation

Self-hypnosis is a powerful tool for individuals navigating the aftermath of childhood trauma, offering a means to access deeper layers of the subconscious and foster healing. It involves guiding oneself into a relaxed and focused state where the mind becomes more receptive to positive suggestions and insights. Trauma survivors often find self-hypnosis particularly beneficial for managing intrusive memories, reducing anxiety, and cultivating a sense of agency over their healing process.

Parts negotiation, a complementary practice often used alongside self-hypnosis, is rooted in the idea that the self is composed of multiple "parts" or facets of identity, each with its own emotional experience and perspective. For those who have experienced childhood trauma, these parts can include inner voices representing fear, anger, or sadness, as well as resilience and hope. Parts negotiation creates a structured dialogue between these facets, allowing individuals to understand the needs and motivations of each part and work toward internal harmony.

Self-hypnosis practice: Begin by creating a calm environment free from distractions. Close your eyes and focus on your breathing, gradually entering a state of relaxation. Use imagery or affirmations to guide your subconscious toward healing goals. For instance, imagine a safe haven where your inner child feels nurtured and protected.

Parts Negotiation: Identify the emotions or inner voices that feel prominent in your experience. Through journaling or visualization, engage with each "part" as if they were distinct personalities, asking questions like "What do you need right now?" or "How can I support you?" This practice encourages collaboration between conflicting parts and integration of the self.

Why It Works: Self-hypnosis and parts negotiation are particularly effective for trauma survivors because they address the fragmented sense of self often associated with unresolved childhood trauma. By entering a hypnotic state, individuals can bypass the conscious mind's defenses and access core beliefs and memories, facilitating profound emotional release and reprocessing. This process enables survivors to reshape narratives surrounding their experiences, fostering empowerment and self-compassion.

Non-clinical therapeutic techniques provide trauma survivors with practical tools to complement traditional psychotherapy. By fostering mind-body connection, emotional regulation, and self-expression, these practices empower individuals to navigate their healing journeys with resilience and self-compassion. With regular practice, these techniques can transform traumatic experiences into opportunities for growth and self-discovery.

Chapter 9 - Clinical Interventions

Psychotherapy (Primary Component)

Dissociative identity disorder is recognized as a complex psychological condition primarily resulting from severe and prolonged childhood trauma. Central to its treatment is psychotherapy, which is acknowledged as the most effective modality for addressing the disorder's dissociative defense mechanisms and fragmented self-concept.

The Benefits of Therapeutic Alliance

A strong therapeutic alliance really makes a difference when treating dissociative disorders and childhood trauma. Studies show that when therapists and clients build a good relationship, people see real improvements, like feeling less dissociated, reducing PTSD symptoms, and greater emotional regulation. This strong connection helps clients function more adaptively and form healthier relationships, making the healing process smoother and more effective.

Patients who rate their therapeutic alliance highly often exhibit notable progress in both psychological and behavioral domains. Research highlights just how crucial it is when therapists and clients collaborate, set goals, and genuinely connect on a personal level. This kind of teamwork is key to building trust and safety, the real foundation for healing and making progress.

The therapeutic alliance also facilitates emotional and physical attunement (a type of co-regulation). Through consistent and affirming interactions, therapists provide validation and empathy, allowing the limbic system, integral in emotion and memory processing, to transition from hypervigilance to a state of calm. This process helps to mitigate stress responses and also establishes neural pathways conducive to resilience and emotional stability.

The therapeutic alliance is more than a relational dynamic; it is a mechanism for profound psychological and neurobiological change. Positive relationships cultivated within the context of therapy serve as transformative environments for the limbic system, the region of the brain intricately involved in emotion, memory, and behavioral regulation. When individuals engage in trusted therapeutic alliances, the limbic system begins to resonate with safety and empathy. This resonance occurs as the therapist mirrors emotional states, offering validation and attunement that soothe the brain's stress responses. Over time, these affirming interactions recalibrate hypervigilant neural pathways, shifting the limbic system from a state of constant alertness to one of grounded calm. Gradual exposure to emotional vulnerability within the therapeutic space allows the limbic system to form new patterns, enabling smoother transitions between states of distress and equilibrium.

Revision, the final transformative aspect of the limbic system within positive relationships, involves the reorganization of emotional memories and self-concept. As therapy delves into trauma narratives, the limbic system begins to reinterpret stored experiences, replacing fear-driven associations with empowered perspectives. The therapist serves as both a witness and a guide, facilitating the integration of fragmented memories and promoting a cohesive sense of identity. This process not only reshapes neurobiological pathways but also instills hope, offering individuals a renewed capacity for healthy relationships and emotional processing beyond the therapeutic setting.

Therapeutic Framework: Phase-Oriented Treatment

The phased approach to psychotherapy for dissociative identity disorder offers a structured framework to address the intricate and often overlapping symptoms of the disorder. By systematically progressing through stages designed to establish safety, process trauma, and promote integration, this method provides individuals with a comprehensive pathway toward healing and stability.

At this point, we should point out that the process of integration is not one where there would be a mushing together of parts, or a blending to the degree that the core identity becomes someone completely new. Integration, in the sense that it is a process of working with those with DID, is a linking together of apparently normal parts and emotional parts. It is the process of communication that involves telling the stories of one's life as told from the perspective of each part, a recognition of the horrific experience, acceptance of what was and what is, and an approach to the future that does not include reliving past trauma.

Phase One: Safety and Stabilization

The initial phase emphasizes establishing safety, building a secure therapeutic alliance, and stabilizing acute symptoms. This stage focuses on emotional regulation, fostering a sense of security, and preparing the individual for subsequent therapeutic interventions.

Phase Two: Confronting and Processing Trauma

This phase centers on addressing compartmentalized traumatic memories and facilitating their integration into the individual's self-narrative. Techniques in this phase seek to help patients gradually process overwhelming experiences without compromising psychological stability.

Phase Three: Identity Integration and Rehabilitation

The final phase aims to promote co-consciousness, inter-identity communication, and integrated functioning among dissociated identities. This process ultimately fosters a unified sense of self while enhancing emotional regulation and overall well-being. If full integration is not the goal, then communication between parts, compassion, and collaboration should be primary.

Approaches to Addressing Dissociative Defense Mechanisms

Psychodynamic psychotherapy remains a central method for treating DID. It involves careful interpretation of dissociative defense mechanisms such as compartmentalization, denial, projection, and amnesia. Therapeutic techniques often include fostering inter-identity communication, utilizing relaxation strategies, and addressing primary dissociative symptoms like depersonalization and identity confusion.

While some therapists engage in direct communication with alternate identities, perspectives differ regarding the extent to which this should be pursued. Certain approaches advocate treating the patient as a cohesive whole rather than focusing exclusively on the multiplicity phenomenon. The approach should be intuitive and dependent upon the needs of the client and the skills of the therapist. Working with each part in a system can be the only way to diminish the impact of past trauma and its 'stuckness.'

Hypnosis, though occasionally employed as an adjunctive

tool for accessing traumatic memories and facilitating communication, is approached cautiously due to concerns over potential iatrogenic effects, including the reinforcement of reconstructed memories that may lack factual accuracy.

Challenges and Controversies

The diagnosis and treatment of DID face several controversies that challenge its management and understanding. Many critics argue that certain therapeutic techniques may inadvertently shape or reinforce symptoms, particularly by encouraging the elaboration of alternate identities. These concerns highlight the importance of employing sensitive and evidence-based approaches to avoid exacerbating the disorder.

Professional doubt regarding the legitimacy of DID also complicates its treatment. Disagreements within the medical community often undermine patient care and delay access to specialized interventions. Such skepticism can negatively impact the support available to individuals struggling with this complex condition. Suppose you are a clinician who does not believe in the validity of dissociative identity disorder. In that case, it may be the best course of action to refer your client to a more specialized trauma therapist or research the condition to a degree to which you are comfortable addressing the unique issues in DID. If you are the one who has DID and your condition is not validated, you may want to search for a more qualified professional. If you are not a trauma therapist but are curious and provide a nonjudgmental space for your clients, by all means, help your client who has DID. If you are an individual with DID, the therapeutic relationship is the most important element of the healing process. The matching of client-therapist is vital.

Misdiagnosis remains another significant challenge in addressing DID. Clinicians frequently mistake it for other psychiatric conditions, such as borderline personality disorder or schizophrenia. This confusion often leads to ineffective treatment strategies and delays in implementing proper care tailored to DID.

Although psychotherapy is widely regarded as the cornerstone of effective DID treatment, its outcomes can vary greatly among individuals. Formal evidence-based treatment guidelines are still unavailable, which adds to the variability in patient results. These challenges emphasize the need for continued research and refinement of therapeutic methods to ensure better outcomes for those affected by DID.

Therapeutic Relationship and Patient Empowerment

A secure and trusting relationship between therapist and patient is integral to recovery. Therapists play a critical role in fostering affective attunement, relational repair, and intersubjective growth, enabling patients to confront and process painful memories in a supportive environment. Furthermore, empowering patients through understanding their dissociative symptoms can facilitate self-awareness, emotional regulation, and eventual integration.

The phased, individualized approach of psychotherapy provides an essential framework for treating dissociative identity disorder. While challenges persist, addressing dissociative defense mechanisms, fostering inter-identity communication, and prioritizing a secure therapeutic alliance remain fundamental to achieving lasting psychological stability and improved quality of life.

Pharmacotherapy (Secondary)

While no specific medications target DID directly, pharmacotherapy provides valuable support in managing associated symptoms. Clinicians often prescribe antidepressants to alleviate depressive symptoms and address post-traumatic stress disorder (PTSD), which frequently co-occurs with DID. Atypical antipsychotics also play a crucial role in stabilizing mood, reducing dissociation, and mitigating hallucinations, thereby offering relief to patients coping with intense psychological challenges. In addition, anxiolytics are used to manage severe anxiety and fear, helping individuals regain emotional balance in stressful situations.

Emerging approaches in pharmacotherapy show promise for addressing dissociative symptoms. Recent evidence highlights the potential benefits of zinc and L-carnosine supplementation, which may reduce the intensity of dissociation and promote greater emotional stability. Novel interventions continue to expand the therapeutic options available to individuals living with DID, complementing existing treatment methods and paving the way for more comprehensive care.

Hypnotherapy

Hypnotherapy has emerged as an adjunctive tool in the treatment of DID and other trauma-related disorders, providing a structured approach to symptom management and facilitating therapeutic communication between dissociative identities. While hypnotherapy's role in treating this complex condition continues to be debated, its potential benefits for symptom relief and trauma integration are noteworthy.

Benefits of Hypnotherapy for Individuals with DID

Hypnotherapy is particularly advantageous for individuals with DID due to its ability to address core aspects of dissociation and trauma. By leveraging the patient's heightened suggestibility, hypnotherapy enables access to fragmented memories and compartmentalized emotions, fostering awareness and communication among distinct personality states. This therapeutic mechanism can alleviate pervasive inter-identity conflict, one of the most challenging aspects of DID, by facilitating a dialogue between alters and promoting emotional reconciliation.

Another benefit lies in its efficacy for managing severe symptoms commonly associated with DID, such as intrusive flashbacks, dissociative hallucinations, and episodes of intense emotional dysregulation. Through guided hypnotic techniques, patients can develop coping strategies to mitigate distress, thereby improving their functionality and quality of life. Furthermore, hypnotherapy's neurobiological grounding, supported by observations of altered neural activity in regions like the hippocampus and prefrontal cortex during posthypnotic states, lends credence to its therapeutic value. Hypnotherapy provides an opportunity to recondition the person's mind into states of safety, emotional calm, and the present moment.

Applications of Hypnotherapy

The application of hypnotherapy in DID treatment is multifaceted, ranging from symptom attenuation to trauma processing. Historically, hypnotherapy has been employed to facilitate the abreaction (body memories) of traumatic events and integrate dissociative memories (bringing trauma out of the past and into the present). Techniques such as ideomotor signaling allow therapists to engage with hidden alters, uncover repressed experiences, and promote co-consciousness among fragmented identities. When used judiciously, hypnotherapy can serve as a catalyst for identity integration, helping patients achieve a cohesive sense of self. The Ericksonian therapeutic method is recommended for those who have experienced sexual abuse and other trauma.

Symptom Management

Current clinical consensus emphasizes hypnotherapy as a tool for reducing severe PTSD-like symptoms, rather than focusing solely on memory recovery. Patients with DID often experience extensive memory fragmentation and amnesia, complicating their ability to narrate traumatic experiences. Hypnotherapy provides a safe avenue for accessing these memories in a controlled environment while suppressing overwhelming emotional responses.

Trauma Integration

For individuals with DID, hypnotherapy facilitates the processing of deeply buried traumatic memories that contribute to identity fragmentation. By bridging the gap between dissociative identities, it fosters an environment of communication and collaboration, enabling patients to confront past traumas without re-traumatization.

Considerations and Cautions

While hypnotherapy offers promising benefits, its application must be approached with caution. The potential for confabulation, mixing facts with fabricated memories during hypnotic states underscores the importance of using hypnotherapy within a structured and evidence-based framework. Similarly, high levels of patient suggestibility necessitate careful management to avoid unintended iatrogenic effects, such as the creation or amplification of dissociative symptoms through suggestive techniques.

Critics of hypnotherapy have raised concerns about its historical misuse, particularly in cases involving recovered memory therapy. However, with proper training and adherence to ethical guidelines, hypnotherapy can be employed as a valuable adjunct to other therapeutic interventions, such as psychodynamic therapy, cognitive behavioral therapy (CBT), and trauma-focused CBT.

Hypnotherapy, when integrated thoughtfully into the

treatment plan for dissociative identity disorder, provides a unique avenue for symptom relief and trauma integration. Its ability to foster communication among fragmented identities, manage distressing symptoms, and enable the processing of traumatic memories underscores its therapeutic potential. While challenges and controversies persist, hypnotherapy remains a viable option for individuals with DID, offering hope for improved outcomes in the management of this complex condition. Continued research and clinical refinement will be crucial in maximizing its efficacy and addressing concerns surrounding its use.

The Application of Internal Family Systems

Internal Family Systems (IFS), developed by Richard Schwartz, presents a remarkably effective and compassionate framework for working with individuals diagnosed with dissociative identity disorder (DID). This therapeutic model conceptualizes the human mind as an internal system of distinct "parts" that interact with one another, all guided by a central "Self." The principles of IFS align closely with the needs of individuals with DID, making it uniquely suited to address the complexities of their condition.

Understanding Internal Family Systems

IFS begins with the understanding that the mind is composed of various "parts," each of which holds unique roles and characteristics. These parts often emerge as adaptive responses to life experiences, and in the case of trauma, they can take on "extreme roles" to protect the system. For example, some parts, referred to as "managers," work proactively to prevent pain, while others, called "firefighters," act impulsively to suppress distress. "Exiles," often the most vulnerable parts, carry the emotional burdens of unresolved trauma. Central to the IFS framework is the "Self," a wise, compassionate, and undamaged core within every individual that has the capacity to lead and heal the system. If these categorizations of parts in IFS sound familiar, it is because they are similar to the identified parts and associated roles in DID. You can think of the managers as the hosts or gatekeepers, the extreme roles may be persecutors or protectors, the exiles could be the child parts (littles).

The Relevance of IFS in DID Treatment

Individuals with DID experience a fracturing of identity into distinct, autonomous "parts" or personality states, each with its own memories, emotions, and roles. This phenomenon closely mirrors the IFS concept of parts, making the model highly compatible with DID treatment. IFS does not pathologize these distinct states but instead views them as adaptive mechanisms developed to cope with overwhelming trauma. This destigmatizing perspective validates the experiences of those with DID and fosters a nonjudgmental therapeutic environment.

Direct Engagement with Parts

A key feature of IFS is its direct, respectful engagement with internal parts, akin to the therapeutic approach of working with parts in DID. Therapists facilitate dialogue between the individual's Self and their parts, allowing each to express its needs, fears, and burdens. For individuals with DID, this approach ensures that all parts are heard and acknowledged, promoting internal cooperation and reducing the chaotic internal conflicts often experienced. By addressing the unique roles and intentions of each part, IFS helps individuals build a cohesive sense of self.

Resolving Internal Conflicts

DID is characterized by pervasive conflict among dissociative identities, stemming from competing emotions, goals, and memories. IFS directly addresses these conflicts by encouraging parts to communicate and collaborate under the guidance of the

Self. This process fosters harmony within the internal system, paving the way for greater co-consciousness and eventual integration of identities.

Processing Trauma

Trauma processing is a cornerstone of DID treatment, and IFS provides a structured and safe framework for this work. Through a process known as "unburdening," parts that carry the weight of traumatic memories are guided to release their pain and transform their roles within the system. This method ensures that trauma is addressed without retraumatization, empowering the individual to move forward with a sense of healing and wholeness. Titration, an in and out of trauma-processing, is the safest, most effective way of promoting intra-part communication, co-consciousness, and integration. The downside: this can take a long time.

Promoting Self-Leadership

One of the most unique and powerful aspects of IFS is its emphasis on cultivating self-leadership. For individuals with DID, this involves helping them differentiate their core self from their parts, allowing the self to take on a leadership role in guiding the system. This shift not only fosters a sense of empowerment but also establishes a stable internal hierarchy, reducing the frequency and intensity of dissociative episodes.

Why IFS Is the Most Appropriate Approach

While other therapeutic models may emphasize symptom management or memory recovery, IFS offers a holistic and integrative approach that aligns with the lived experiences of individuals with DID. Its non-pathologizing view of parts validates their purpose as protective mechanisms rather than symptoms to be eliminated. Additionally, IFS prioritizes the individual's innate capacity for healing through themselves, empowering them to take an active role in their recovery.

IFS also addresses many of the concerns raised in DID treatment. For instance, its structured process minimizes the risks of suggestibility and confabulation, ensuring that therapy remains grounded in the client's authentic experiences. Moreover, the model's focus on collaboration rather than confrontation with parts reduces the risk of retraumatization or the inadvertent reinforcement of dissociative symptoms.

Challenges and Considerations

While IFS offers immense potential, its application requires careful consideration. Therapists must be well-trained in the model to navigate the complexities of working with highly dissociative clients. Additionally, ensuring safety and stabilization in the early stages of treatment is critical to prevent overwhelming the internal system.

Internal Family Systems stands out as a compassionate and effective approach to therapy for individuals with dissociative identity disorder. By fostering dialogue between parts, resolving internal conflicts, processing trauma, and promoting self-leadership, IFS offers a path toward integration and healing. Its alignment with the experiences and needs of those with DID verifies its appropriateness as a therapeutic model, offering hope for meaningful recovery and enhanced quality of life.

Traditional Understanding Identity Integration

While the traditional view of integration often prioritizes the development of a unified self as the primary goal of therapy, integration does not necessarily have to mean merging all parts into one. Instead, it can be reconceptualized as a process of fostering connections, enhancing communication among parts, and facilitating the sharing of memories. This perspective allows therapy to support collaboration and understanding within the internal system without compromising the distinct roles and identities of individual parts.

When the primary goal is to create a cohesive sense of self by incorporating dissociative identities into a core identity, therapy enables individuals to weave fragmented aspects of their personality into a unified sense of being. This process not only fosters deeper connections with one's personal history but also helps individuals access and reconcile emotional states that were previously compartmentalized. By promoting integration (in terms of linking parts), therapy provides the tools to build a stable and harmonious internal framework, empowering individuals to move toward a more balanced and fulfilling life.

Resolution of Internal Conflict

Patients with DID often experience profound internal conflicts stemming from differing values, goals, and emotional states across their identities. Therapy seeks to explore these conflicts and foster resolution, promoting a sense of harmony among the various parts of the self.

Enhancement of Co-Consciousness and Communication

Integration necessitates an increased level of co-consciousness and improved communication among dissociative identities. By bridging gaps in awareness and understanding, therapy supports a collaborative and functional internal system.

Unburdening and Reharmonizing Internal Systems

Approaches such as Internal Family Systems (IFS) play a pivotal role in unburdening parts of the self weighed down by traumatic experiences. Through this process, these parts are redefined in ways that promote their positive contributions, ensuring a balanced and harmonious system.

EMDR

The International Society for the Study of Trauma and Dissociation (ISSTD) Guidelines explicitly state that EMDR (Eye Movement Desensitization and Reprocessing) is not recommended for individuals with dissociative identity disorder until thorough stabilization across all dissociative self-states has been achieved. This recommendation is based on the potential risks of destabilization and exacerbation of dissociative symptoms. Although neurobiological contraindications have not been substantiated through high-level reviews or meta-analyses, expert opinion and clinical consensus highlight concerns such as the possibility of switching between identity states, amnesia, and symptom aggravation.

Key points from the literature further support the phased approach outlined in the ISSTD Guidelines, which includes stabilization, trauma processing, and eventual integration. Trauma-focused interventions like EMDR should only be initiated after stabilization and affect-regulation skills have been effectively established across all parts, including both the apparently normal parts (ANP) and emotional parts (EP). Clinical consensus emphasizes that initiating EMDR prematurely may lead to increased internal conflicts, switching between identity states, and heightened risks of self-harm.

Although EMDR is widely recognized as a first-line treatment for straightforward PTSD, international guidelines such as those from the World Health Organization (WHO) and the American Psychological Association (APA) advise caution or exclusion of its use in complex dissociative cases like DID. Clinical reports and expert reviews highlight the potential destabilizing effects of EMDR, particularly its bilateral stimulation (BLS) component, which may inadvertently reinforce compartmentalized trauma fragments. While theoretical papers propose neurobiological mechanisms for these risks, empirical evidence remains limited and is primarily based on case studies and expert opinions.

To mitigate these risks, adapted EMDR protocols for DID have been suggested in practice reports. These adaptations emphasize the necessity of extended stabilization, including resource-building, ego-state or parts work, and containment strategies. However, these protocols are not universally accepted, and all caution against the potential risks associated with EMDR in DID, echoing the ISSTD Guidelines.

The ISSTD Guidelines remain the most authoritative source on the use of EMDR for DID, advocating for a delayed and adapted approach post-stabilization. While clinical case series and theoretical considerations provide valuable insights for protocol design, they do not substitute the evidence level of systematic reviews or meta-analyses. Clinicians are urged to approach EMDR in DID cases with specialized training and an awareness of the unique risks presented by this complex disorder.

Somatic Therapy for Dissociative Identity Disorder

Somatic therapy, an increasingly recognized approach in the treatment of trauma-related disorders, offers promising interventions for individuals with dissociative identity disorder (DID). These therapies, which emphasize body-focused mindfulness and sensory integration, have demonstrated reductions in dissociation, improvements in body awareness, and alleviation of trauma-related distress among survivors of early childhood abuse. While direct evidence specifically targeting DID remains limited, research on somatic interventions for trauma survivors provides valuable insights into their therapeutic potential.

Dr. Peter Levine remains the seminal psychologist in somatoform therapeutic approaches. He emphasizes the need for survivors of trauma to physically work out the unresolved trauma responses that remain stuck in the neurological mechanisms of the body. Dr. Levine posits that humans are the only animals that do not physically release the energy created in traumatic situations, leaving humans vulnerable to re-experiencing the physical abreactions in a repetitive nature. For instance, if someone, we'll call him Tom, was in a car accident and there was a distinct sound of glass breaking, and Tom was trapped in the car. Tom's stress response system would go into flight, fight, and freeze. Tom then has random moments of tightness in his arms, chest, and back, as if he is still stuck. With the aid of somatoform therapy, Tom would be guided through his accident and directed to physically complete the process of getting out of the car, pushing with his arms, chest, and back to open the door. When this process is complete, Tom will have completed the traumatic event and released the energy trapped in his body. For more information on this type of therapeutic approach, you can find Dr. Levine's book, well, everywhere. I highly recommend his book, *"Waking the Tiger."*

Key Therapeutic Approaches and Findings

Somatic therapy encompasses a variety of methods tailored to the needs of individuals grappling with deeply embedded trauma. Sensorimotor Psychotherapy (SP), for instance, offers a structured and phased protocol that focuses on stabilization, trauma processing, and integration. Clinical trials have shown significant improvements in body awareness, anxiety reduction, and dissociation among participants, particularly women with histories of childhood abuse. These outcomes underscore the benefits of body-oriented therapies combining touch and body literacy exercises, which encourage psychological and physical healing.

Trauma-Sensitive Yoga (TCTSY), another somatic intervention, has been validated in randomized controlled trials for individuals suffering from chronic PTSD due to childhood abuse. This approach not only facilitates emotional regulation but also enhances interoceptive awareness, a critical component in reconnecting individuals with their bodies. Studies have revealed remission rates that are nearly double those of control groups, with participants reporting improved quality of life and greater ability to tolerate affective distress.

Innovative methods, such as vibroacoustic (low-frequency sound vibrations) feedback integrated into mindfulness practices, are also emerging as effective tools for enhancing interoception and reducing dissociation. Some of these therapies use chest vibrations along with mindful breathing to help people really tune into their bodies. This combo can boost heart rate variability, sharpen focus, and even strengthen brain connections. While these early results are promising, we still need more research to truly understand how and why these benefits happen.

Movement and dance-based therapies demonstrate encouraging results in the narrative and case study literature. These interventions often address dissociation through pacing, body mapping, and corrective somatic experiences, providing individuals with opportunities to reengage with their physical selves. Similarly, psychomotor therapy programs, such as "Feel-Own-Move," have shown promise in trauma shelter populations, helping participants ground their experiences through phased movement, trauma-sensitive touch, and guided imagery. Arts-based and Gestalt-inspired body mindfulness also contribute to improving body perception, though systematic evaluations of these therapies remain sparse.

Critical Limitations and Gaps

Despite the promising evidence surrounding somatic therapy, several critical gaps persist in the research. Direct evidence specifically focused on DID is scarce, with most studies concentrating on adults with PTSD and histories of abuse. Insights into DID are primarily derived from narrative accounts and case reports, lacking the robust quantitative data necessary for establishing best practices. Process data and prognosis metrics often remain underreported. While phased interventions have been outlined, granular details such as titration schedules, identity state mapping, and long-term outcomes are frequently omitted.

Another challenge lies in the generalizability of existing findings. The effectiveness of somatic therapies can vary based on trauma modality, initial levels of dissociation, group versus individual settings, and the expertise of facilitators. These moderators require further systematic investigation to ensure that therapeutic approaches are tailored appropriately to the needs of DID populations.

Future Directions

Looking ahead, the field must strive for rigorous, methodologically sound studies that explicitly include DID populations. These studies should report detailed metrics on phased somatic intervention processes while exploring long-term outcomes. Additionally, the integration of novel somatic augmentations, such as vibroacoustic feedback, warrants deeper investigation to elucidate their mechanisms and optimize their application in DID treatment.

Somatic therapy holds immense potential for addressing the complex challenges presented by DID. Among the best-supported interventions are structured, body-focused group therapies, such as Sensorimotor Psychotherapy adaptations, and Trauma-Sensitive

Yoga, both of which have demonstrated effectiveness in reducing dissociation and improving body awareness. By embracing innovative techniques and addressing the critical gaps in research, the therapeutic community can advance its understanding of somatic interventions and provide more comprehensive support to individuals with DID, fostering both stability and long-term recovery.

Cognitive Behavior Therapy for DID Diagnosis

Cognitive Behavioral Therapy (CBT) is a widely recognized and evidence-based therapeutic modality that focuses on the interplay between thoughts, emotions, and behaviors. At its core, CBT seeks to identify and challenge maladaptive thought patterns that contribute to emotional distress and unhealthy behaviors. By encouraging individuals to reframe their perspectives, CBT enables them to develop healthier coping mechanisms and achieve greater psychological resilience. Structured and goal-oriented, this approach is often tailored to the specific needs of clients, making it a versatile and effective tool for addressing a range of mental health challenges.

CBT works particularly well for individuals who have experienced trauma, including those diagnosed with post-traumatic stress disorder (PTSD) or dissociative identity disorder (DID). Trauma often disrupts cognitive processes, leading to persistent negative beliefs, heightened emotional reactivity, and avoidance behaviors. CBT provides a framework for understanding these patterns and introduces strategies for managing them. For clients with PTSD, CBT techniques such as exposure therapy help reduce the intensity of fear responses by gradually confronting traumatic memories in a controlled and safe environment. Similarly, cognitive restructuring allows individuals to reframe distorted beliefs about themselves and their experiences, fostering a sense of empowerment and self-worth.

The effectiveness of CBT for trauma-related conditions lies in its active and collaborative nature. It encourages clients to engage directly with their thoughts and behaviors, fostering a sense of agency over their recovery journey. For individuals with DID, CBT's structured strategies can facilitate communication between fragmented identity states and promote emotional regulation. By addressing the root cognitive distortions that fuel dissociation, CBT helps individuals build a more cohesive sense of self. This approach also integrates techniques for grounding and mindfulness, which are essential for reconnecting clients with their physical and emotional experiences. Such interventions counteract the feelings of disconnection that often accompany trauma.

CBT's success is further driven by its adaptability and emphasis on measurable outcomes. Therapists work alongside clients to set clear, attainable goals, ensuring progress is tracked and celebrated. This outcome-oriented framework is particularly beneficial for trauma survivors, as it provides a tangible sense of achievement and forward momentum. CBT's structured methods can be customized to address individual needs, whether through group sessions, individual therapy, or integrated approaches that combine CBT with complementary modalities. By offering a pathway to reclaim control over thoughts and feelings, CBT empowers trauma survivors to move beyond pain and toward a fulfilling life.

Integrative Therapeutic Approach

Integrative therapy for dissociative identity disorder (DID) emphasizes the importance of tailoring treatment approaches to meet the unique needs of each individual. This method blends a variety of therapeutic modalities, such as cognitive-behavioral therapy, hypnotherapy, somatic therapy, and psychodynamic approaches, among others, to create a comprehensive and adaptable framework. The goal is to address the multifaceted symptoms of DID, such as dissociative amnesia, identity fragmentation, and affective disturbances, while fostering a sense of safety and trust between therapists and clients.

The importance of an integrative approach lies in its ability to provide flexibility and responsiveness to the complex challenges presented by DID. No single therapeutic modality can encompass the full scope of this disorder's manifestations, making it critical to draw upon multiple techniques to support healing. For instance, hypnotherapy may be used to access and process traumatic memories that underpin dissociative episodes, while somatic therapy can help clients reconnect with their bodies and reduce physical manifestations of trauma, such as chronic tension or unexplained pain. Cognitive-behavioral strategies may assist in restructuring negative thought patterns, while psychodynamic therapy may delve into the roots of dissociation and provide insight into unconscious processes.

The integrative approach is most effective because it honors the uniqueness of each client's experience. DID is not a monolithic condition; its presentation and impact vary widely from one individual to another. By customizing treatment plans that incorporate elements from different modalities, clinicians can address specific needs, such as facilitating communication between dissociated identity states, developing healthy coping mechanisms, and promoting emotional regulation. Personalized care fosters greater rapport and trust, empowering clients on their journey toward recovery.

Speaking directly to those who have experience trauma: the integrative therapy works best when you and your therapist share the same goals and build a strong, trusting relationship. Mixing different approaches can be especially helpful, and teamwork among therapists, psychiatrists, and other care providers makes sure you get the support you need. By taking this team-based, holistic view, therapists can pay attention to both your mental and physical well-being. When therapists meet DID's challenges head-on with a variety of tools, they're able to help you find stability and even thrive.

Challenges in Treatment and Diagnosis

Recovery from DID is possible, and many individuals diagnosed with this condition can lead fulfilling lives with appropriate therapeutic intervention. However, the path to recovery is often arduous and lengthy, requiring a nuanced approach tailored to the needs of each individual. The chronic nature of DID and its intricate symptoms present challenges in treatment and diagnosis. Many individuals with DID often have extended histories within the mental health system without experiencing adequate treatment responses before receiving an accurate diagnosis. This delay in recognition can hinder progress and exacerbate existing difficulties.

The complexity of dissociative symptoms, which may not initially appear distinct, contributes to the frequent misdiagnosis or underdiagnosis of DID. The absence of formal, evidence-based treatment guidelines specifically designed for DID poses challenges for clinicians. While individual psychodynamic psychotherapy is widely employed, its efficacy varies depending on the patient and the therapeutic approach used. Skepticism and professional doubt surrounding the diagnosis can lead to patients experiencing iatrogenic doubt, therapist-induced uncertainty about their own experiences. This phenomenon can further harm their already fractured sense of self and create barriers to accessing specialized care.

Despite these challenges, it is essential to acknowledge that DID can be managed effectively with the right therapeutic strategies. A professional commitment to understanding the disorder, coupled with compassionate and tailored interventions, offers hope for individuals navigating the complexities of dissociative identity states and their recovery journey.

Factors Influencing Prognosis
The prognosis for individuals with dissociative identity disorder can be significantly influenced by various factors. One of the critical determinants is early and accurate diagnosis. Identifying DID early makes a real difference; it helps protect people from more trauma and gets treatment started sooner and more smoothly. Taking this first step sets up a recovery path that's both doable and meaningful.

The commitment and motivation of the patient, combined with the expertise and support of mental health professionals, are vital components in shaping a positive prognosis. When people stick with their therapy and have caring, knowledgeable providers who really understand trauma and dissociation, they're much more likely to see real progress. The therapeutic alliance, built on trust and mutual understanding, serves as a cornerstone for addressing complex dissociative symptoms.

Emerging research also points to potential neurobiological correlations that may influence recovery. Studies suggest that interventions such as phase-oriented psychotherapy and targeted medication could lead to an increase or recovery in hippocampal volume, although the implications of these findings are not yet fully understood. This area of study highlights the need for continued exploration to deepen our understanding of the biological underpinnings of DID and refine treatment methodologies. Continued research is essential not only to improve diagnostic precision but also to enhance therapeutic techniques, ensuring that individuals living with DID have access to interventions that foster healing, self-awareness, and emotional stability.

Therapeutic Interventions and Emotional Regulation for Recovery

Feeling less emotional distress plays a complicated but important role in how people with dissociative disorders, like dissociative fugue or amnesia, recover and heal. For many, stress and anxiety show up alongside tough memories and trauma, making things more challenging. Dissociation acts almost like a shield, helping people put some distance between themselves and the pain of what happened. While that defense can help in the short term, it sometimes breaks down, letting painful memories and feelings come back into focus and making recovery more challenging. Navigating this up-and-down process is a key part of working through dissociative disorders.

Therapeutic interventions emerge as a cornerstone in addressing emotional distress and fostering recovery. Establishing safe and trusting therapeutic relationships enables patients to confront and process fragmented or painful memories. Through such relationships, individuals can develop the capacity to identify, understand, and tolerate previously dissociated emotions, gradually reducing inner turmoil. Therapy often focuses on reconciling internal conflicts and addressing dissociative mechanisms, aiming to decrease both primary dissociative symptoms, such as amnesia, and secondary symptoms, such as distress linked to fragmented identities. Approaches like Internal Family Systems therapy facilitate compassionate engagement with "parts" of the self, enabling emotional release and transformation, which contributes to overall distress reduction.

On a neurobiological level, recovery from dissociative conditions is associated with notable changes. For instance, studies have documented increased hippocampal volume in individuals who achieved recovery after therapy. These neurobiological findings align with observations of cognitive improvements associated with the reintegration of neural networks linked to memory functions.

Natural and easy fixes are often overlooked, but the research is clear: improved sleep, consistent exercise, and good nutrition are foundations for improving all mental health disorders. Research indicates that improved sleep patterns are independently linked to reductions in dissociative symptoms. When a healthy lifestyle is implemented, hormones become more balanced, foggy thinking becomes clearer, and emotional regulation is easier to manage. Comprehensive therapeutic approaches, in conjunction with lifestyle changes, address both emotional and cognitive dimensions, supported by neurobiological insights, and offer the most promising path toward recovery.

Ambivalence in the Recovery Process

Recovery from dissociative disorders, including dissociative identity disorder (DID) and dissociative amnesia (DA), is often described as a challenging and ambivalent journey. This process is marked by internal conflicts and external relational interactions, where individuals grapple with fragmented aspects of their identity and memory. One illustrative case describes a patient who experienced an internal struggle between a part that acknowledged past abuse and another, more fearful part that resisted this knowledge. Through therapy, the "understanding" part of the patient gradually strengthened, while the "fearful" part diminished. This highlights the unpredictable and non-linear nature of recovery.

A significant element of this ambivalence arises in relation to memory retrieval. Many individuals in recovery are hesitant about accessing dissociated memories due to fears of confronting overwhelming and painful past experiences. Even when cognitive functioning shows improvement, amnesia often persists, likely due to protective defense mechanisms such as neuronal inhibition. These mechanisms serve to shield individuals from re-experiencing intense emotional distress. Recovery, therefore, is not typically perceived as a definitive endpoint but rather as an ongoing process where individuals develop an increasing capacity to hold and reflect on their experiences in consciousness.

Challenges in Accessing Care

Despite advancements in understanding dissociative disorders, many individuals face significant barriers to accessing effective care. Professional skepticism and a lack of consensus around diagnoses like DID can lead to iatrogenic doubting, where patients internalize doubt about their own experiences, further damaging their sense of self. Systemic inconsistencies in diagnostic rigor and treatment availability exacerbate these challenges, often leaving patients without adequate support. Addressing these barriers requires awareness, education, and systemic changes to ensure access to care.

While recovery is achievable, it requires a combination of therapeutic interventions, supportive relationships, and systemic improvements to overcome the challenges inherent to these conditions. Continued research and tailored care models are essential to refining treatments and providing hope for individuals navigating the intricate pathways of dissociation and healing.

The prognosis and recovery journey for individuals with DID often involve extensive and carefully tailored therapeutic intervention. With the correct support, individuals diagnosed with DID have shown the capacity to recover and lead rewarding lives. However, this path is typically lengthy and fraught with challenges.

The complexities of DID often result in delays in diagnosis, with many individuals navigating the mental health system for extended periods before receiving an accurate identification of their condition. Misdiagnosis or underdiagnosis frequently occurs due to the subtlety of dissociative symptoms, which may not be immediately apparent. Furthermore, the absence of formal, evidence-based treatment guidelines specifically designed for DID adds an additional layer of complexity to its management. The contested nature of the disorder within the professional community can introduce skepticism and doubt for both patients and clinicians, further complicating access to effective care.

Therapeutic strategies for DID emphasize fostering communication and cooperation between dissociative identity states. The therapeutic process frequently involves assisting patients in processing traumatic experiences, addressing defensive mechanisms like amnesia and splitting, and integrating somatic experiences. Pharmacotherapy can complement psychotherapy in managing comorbid conditions such as depression and anxiety, while specialized approaches such as Cognitive Behavioral Therapy (CBT), schema (multi-phase) therapy, hypnotherapy, and internal family systems therapy are noted for their efficacy in addressing specific aspects of the disorder.

Limitations and Gaps in Understanding Identity States in DID

There is currently no single scholarly work that integrates diverse perspectives: neurobiological, psychological, clinical, trigger-based, and phenomenological into a unified and comprehensive review. Existing studies have excelled in exploring the neurobiological aspects of DID, but often lack depth in capturing its first-person experiences and clinical nuances. Thus, the field would benefit greatly from research that bridges these critical gaps, offering a multidimensional understanding of identity states in DID.

Some studies have touched on triggers and personal experiences of switching between identity states in dissociative identity disorder (DID), but there's still a big gap when it comes to exploring these areas in detail. While the topic has been mentioned in overviews, the finer details are pretty scarce. Things like autonomic and neuroendocrine markers, or the subtle clinical changes leading up to these state transitions, haven't been thoroughly explored either.

ABOUT THE AUTHOR

Amy Rouleau, Ph.D., is a distinguished expert in early childhood trauma, the identification and response to human trafficking, dissociative disorders, therapeutic interventions, and the science of happiness. With an impressive career dedicated to education, advocacy, and healing, Amy's work has profoundly impacted individuals and communities alike.

As a psychology professor at both the University of Michigan and Baker College, Amy is passionate about educating the next generation of professionals in her fields of expertise. Her dynamic teaching style and depth of knowledge make her an invaluable asset to her students and colleagues.

Beyond academia, Amy is a sought-after public speaker, known for her ability to engage and inspire audiences at conferences, seminars, and events. Her speaking engagements often cover a wide range of critical topics, including trauma recovery, emotional resilience, and fostering happiness. She is also a published author, whose works contribute to the growing body of knowledge in her areas of specialization.

Amy's personal life is as vibrant as her professional one. She is the proud parent of two wonderful adult children and the delighted grandparent of one grandchild. Her household is filled with the joyous energy of her many four-legged family members. In her leisure time, Amy enjoys oil painting and playing the piano, pursuits that reflect her creative and introspective nature.

For those interested in bringing Amy's expertise and passion to their next event, she can be contacted via email at amyjoypresents@gmail.com. Additional information about her work and speaking engagements can be found on her website at www.amyjoypresents.com.

Amy Rouleau's unique blend of knowledge, compassion, and enthusiasm makes her a truly exceptional educator, speaker, and advocate for positive change.

Check out Amy's books on Amazon.com

Him, Me, and V by Amy Joy
Human Trafficking 101: Stories, Stats, and Solutions by Amy Joy
Write Your Story: A Guided Journal for Healing Trauma by Amy Joy

References

Anda, R. F., Felitti, V. J., Bremner, J. D., Walker, J. D., Whitfield, C., Perry, B. D., Dube, S. R., & Giles, W. H. (2005). The enduring effects of abuse and related adverse experiences in childhood: A convergence of evidence of neurobiology and epidemiology. *Eur Arch Psychiatry Clin Neurosci, 256*, 174-186.

Barlow, M. R. & Chu, J. A. (2014). Measuring fragmentation in Dissociative identity disorder: the integration measure and relationship to switching and time in therapy. *European Journal of Psychotraumatology, 5*.

Berry, K., Fleming, P., Wong, S., & Bucci, S. (2017). Associations between trauma, dissociation, adult attachment and proneness to hallucinations. *Behavioural and Cognitive Psychotherapy, 46*, 292-301.

Berry, K., Varese, F., & Bucci, S. (2017). Cognitive attachment model of voices: evidence base and future implications. *Hypothesis and Theory, 8*(111).

Blihar, D., Crisafio, A., Delgado, E., Buryak, M., Gonzalez, M., & Waechter, R. (2021). A meta-analysis of hippocampal and amygdala volumes in patients diagnosed with Dissociative identity disorder. *Journal of Trauma & Dissociation, 22*(3), 365–377. https://doi.org/10.1080/15299732.2020.1869650

Blihar, D., Delgado, E., Buryak, M., Gonzalez, M., & Waechter, R. (2020). A systematic review of the neuroanatomy of Dissociative identity disorder. *European Journal of Trauma &*

Dissociation, 4(3), 100148–100148. https://doi.org/10.1016/j.ejtd.2020.100148

Bloomfield, M. A. P., Chang, T., Woodl, M. J., Lyons, L. M., Cheng, Z., Bauer-Staeb, C., Hobbs, C., Bracke, S., Kennerly, H., Isham, L., Bewin, C., Billings, J., Greene, T., & Lewis, G. (2021). Psychological processes mediating the association between development trauma and specific psychotic symptoms in adults: a systematic review and meta-analysis. *World Psychiatry, 20*(1), 107-123.

Boyd, J. E., Protopopescu, A., Lanuis, R. A., O'Connor, C., Jetly, R., & McKinnon, M. C. (2020). The contribution of emotion regulation difftculties and dissociative symptoms to functional impairment among civilian inpatients with posttraumatic stress symptoms. *American Psychiatric Association.*

Brandfield, B. (2012). Intersubjectivity and the knowing of inner experience: Finding space for a psychoanalytic phenomenology in research. *Journal of Humanistic Psychology, 53*(3), 263-282.

Brand., B. L. & Chasson, G. S. (2014). Distinguishing simulated from genuine Dissociative identity disorder on the MMPI-2. *Psychological Trauma: Theory, Practice, and Policy, 7*(1), 93-101.

Brand, B. L., Lowenstein, R. J., Lanuis, R., Pain, C., Myrick, A. C., Classen, C. C., McNary, S. W., & Putman, F. W. (2012). A survey of practices and recommended treatment interventions among expert therapists treating patients with Dissociative identity disorder and dissociative disorder not otherwise specified. *Psychological Trauma: Trauma, Theory,*

Research, Practice, and Policy, 4(5), 490-500.

Brand, B., Loewenstein, R. J. & Spiegel, D. (2013). Disinformation about dissociation. *The Journal of Nervous and Mental Disease, 201* (4), 354-356. https://doi.org.10.1097/NMD.0b013e318288d2ee

Brand, B., Loewenstein, R. J. & Spiegel, D. (2014). Dispelling myths about Dissociative identity disorder treatment: An empirically based approach. *Psychiatry, 77*(2).

Brand, B. L., McNary, S. W., Classen, C. C., Loewenstein, R. J., Myrick A. C., Lanius, R., & Rain, C. (2013). A longitudinal naturalistic study of patients with dissociative disorders treated by community clinicians. *Psychological Trauma: Theory, Research, Practice, and Policy, 5*(4), 301-308.

Bremner, J. D. (2006). Traumatic stress: effects on the brain. *Dialogues in Clinical Neuroscience, 8*(4), 445-461.

Bucci, M., Marques, S. S., Oh, D., & Harris, N. B. (2016). Toxic stress in children and adolescents. *Advances in Pediatrics*.

Burnand, G. (2013). A right hemisphere safety backup at work: Hypotheses for deep hypnosis, post-traumatic stress disorder, and dissociation identity disorder. *Medical Hypotheses, 81*(3), 383–388. https://doi.org/10.1016/j.mehy.2013.05.026

Chu, Q., Chong Wu, I. H., Tang, M., Tsoh, J., & Lu, Q. (2020). Temporal relationship of posttraumatic stress disorder symptom clusters during and after an expressive writing intervention for Chinese American breast cancer survivors. *Journal of Psychosomatic Research, 135*.

Classen, C. C., Hughes, L., Clark, C., Hill Mohammed, B., Woods, P., &

Beckett, B. (2020). A pilot RCT of a body-oriented group therapy for complex trauma survivors: An adaptation of sensorimotor psychotherapy. *Journal of Trauma & Dissociation, 22*(1), 52–68. https://doi.org/10.1080/15299732.2020.1760173

Cronin, E., Brand, B. L., & Mattanah, J. F. (2014). The impact of the therapeutic alliance on treatment outcome in patients with dissociative disorders. *European Journal of Psychotraumatology, 5*.

D'Andrea, W., Pole, N., DePierro, J., Freed, S., & Wallace D. B. (2013). Heterogeneity of defensive responses after exposure to trauma: Blunted autonomic reactivity in response to startling sounds. *International Journal of Psychophysiology, 90*, 80-89.

Dalenberg, C., Loewenstein, R., Spiegel, D., Brewin, C., Lanius, R., Frankel, S., Gold, S., Van der Kolk, B., Simeon, D., Vermetten, E., Butler, L., Koopman, C., Courtois, C., Dell, P., Nijenhuis, E., Chu, J., Sar, V., Palesh, O., Cuevas, C., & Paulson, K. (2007). Scientific study of the dissociative disorders. *Psychotherapy and Psychosomatics, 76*(6), 400–401. https://doi.org/10.1159/000107570

Danese, A. & Lewis, S. J. (2017). Psychoneuroimmunology of early-life stress: the hidden wounds of childhood trauma? *Neurpsychopharmacology, 42*, 99-114.

Daniels, J. K., Timmerman, M. E., Spitzer, C., & Lampe, A. (2024). Differential constellations of dissociative symptoms and their association with childhood trauma – a latent profile analysis. *European Journal of Psychotraumatology, 15*(1), 2348345–2348345. https://doi.org/10.1080/20008066.2024.2348345

Demirkol, M. E., Ugur, K., & Tamam, L. (2020). The mediating effects of psychache and dissociation in the relationship between childhood trauma and suicide attempts. *Anadolu psikiyatri dergisi, 21*(5), 453-. https://doi.org/10.5455/apd.82990

Dimitrova, L. I., Chalavi, S., Vissia, E. M., Barker, G. J., Perez, D. L., Veltman, D. J., Diez, I., & Reinders, A. A. T. S. (2025). Brain white matter structural connectivity of trauma and trauma-related dissociation disorders and symptoms. *Psychiatry Research, 346*, 116383-. https://doi.org/10.1016/j.psychres.2025.116383

Dimitrova, L. I., Dean, S. L., Schlumpf, Y. R., Vissia, E. M., Nijenhuis, E. R. S., Chatzi, V., Jäncke, L., Veltman, D. J., Chalavi, S., & Antje A T S Reinders. (2023). A neurostructural biomarker of dissociative amnesia: a hippocampal study in Dissociative identity disorder. *Psychological Medicine, 53*(3), 805–813. https://doi.org/10.1017/S0033291721002154

Dimitrova, L., Fernando, V., Vissia, E. M., Nijenhuis, E. R. S., Draijer, N., & Reinders, A. A. T. S. (2020). Sleep, trauma, fantasy and cognition in Dissociative identity disorder, post-traumatic stress disorder and healthy controls: a replication and extension study. *European Journal of Psychotraumatology, 11*(1), 1705599–1705599. https://doi.org/10.1080/20008198.2019.1705599

Dorahy, M. J., Corry, M., Black, R., Matheson, L., Coles, H., Curran, D., Seager, L., Middleton, W., & Dyer, K. F. W. (2017). Shame, dissociation, and complex PTSD symptoms in traumatized psychiatric and control groups: Direct and indirect associations with relationship distress. *Journal of Clinical Psychology, 73*(4), 439-448.

Ducharme, E. L. (2017). Best practices in working with complex trauma and Dissociative identity disorder. *American Psychiatric Association*.

Duchin, A. & Wiseman, H. (2019). Memoirs of child survivors of the Holocaust: processing and healing of trauma through writing. *Qualitative Psychology, 6*(3), 280-296.

Eagle, M. N. (2017). Attachment theory and research and clinical work. *Psychoanalytic Inquiry, 37*(5), 284-297.

Eisen, M. L., Qin, J., Goodman, G. S., Davis, S., & Crayton, J. (2007). Maltreatment children's memory: accuracy, suggestibility, and psychopathology. *Developmental Psychology, 43*(6), 1275-1294.

Ellason, J. W., Ross, C. A., & Fuchs, D. L. (1996). Lifetime Axis I and II comorbidity and childhood trauma history in Dissociative identity disorder. *Psychiatry (Washington, D.C.), 59*(3), 255–266. https://doi.org/10.1080/00332747.1996.11024766

Ensink, K., Berthelot, N., Begin, M., Maheux, J., & Normandin, L. (2017). Dissociation mediates the relationship between sexual abuse and child psychological difficulties. *Child Abuse & Neglect, 69*, 116-124.

Fani, N., Guelfo, A., La Barrie, D. L., Teer, A. P., Clendinen, C., Karimzadeh, L., Siegle, G. J. (2023). Neurophysiological changes associated with vibroacoustically-augmented breath-focused mindfulness for dissociation: targeting interoception and attention. *Psychological Medicine, 53*(16), 7550–7560. https://doi.org.10.1017/S003329172300127 7

Fedai, U. A., & Asoglu, M. (2022). Analysis of demographic and clinical characteristics of patients with Dissociative identity disorder. *Neuropsychiatric Disease and Treatment, 18,* 3035–3044. https://doi.org/10.2147/NDT.S386648

Fisher, H. L., Craig, T. L., Fearon, P., Morgan, K., Dazzan, P., Lappin, J., Hutchinson, G., Doody, G. A., Jones, P. B., McGuffin, P., Murray, R. M., Leff, J., & Morgan, C. (2011). Reliability and comparability of psychosis patients' retrospective reports of childhood abuse. *Schizophrenia Bulletin, 37*(3), 546-553.

Floris, J., & McPherson, S. (2015). Fighting the whole system: Dissociative identity disorder, labeling theory, and iatrogenic doubting. *Journal of Trauma & Dissociation, 16*(4), 476–493. https://doi.org/10.1080/15299732.2014.990075

Fox, J., Bell, H., Jacobson, L., & Hundley, G. (2013). Recovering identity: A qualitative investigation of a survivor of Dissociative identity disorder. *Journal of Mental Health Counseling, 35*(4), 324–341. https://doi.org/10.17744/mehc.35.4.g715qt65qm281117

Freud, S. (1910). The origin of development of psychoanalysis. *The American Journal of Psychology, 21*(2), 181-218.

Fung, H. W., Chien, W. T., Chan, C., & Ross, C. A. (2023). A cross-cultural investigation of the association between betrayal trauma and dissociative features. *Journal of Interpersonal Violence, 38*(1–2), 1630–1653. https://doi.org/10.1177/08862605221090568

Ganaway, G. K. (1995). Hypnosis, childhood trauma, and Dissociative identity disorder: Toward an integrative theory. *International Journal of Clinical and Experimental Hypnosis, 43*(2), 127–144. https://doi.org/10.1080/00207149508409957

García Vázquez, P., Seijo Zazo, E., Vilellla Martin, C., Serrano García, A., Franch Pato, C. M., Martína Gil, E., & Alvarez Vazquez, C. (2023). An interesting clinical case. New therapies in Dissociative identity disorder. *European Psychiatry, 66*(S1), S970–S971. https://doi.org/10.1192/j.eurpsy.2023.2064

Gerge, A. (2020). What neuroscience and neurofeedback can teach psychotherapists in the field of complex trauma: Interoception, neuroception and the embodiment of unspeakable events in treatment of complex PTSD, dissociative disorders and childhood traumatization. *European Journal of Trauma & Dissociation, 4.*

Giovanardi, G., Vitelli, R., Vergano, C. M., Fortunato, A., Chianura, L., Lingiardi, V., & Speranza, A. M. (2018). Attachment patterns and complex trauma in a sample of adults diagnosed with gender dysphoria. *Frontiers in Psychology, 9*(60).

Giudice, M. D., Ellis, B. J., Hinnant, J. B., & El-Sheikh, M. (2012). Adaptive patterns of stress responsivity: a preliminary investigation. *Development Psychology, 48*(3), 775-790.

Gold, S. N. (2008). The relevance of trauma to general clinical practice. *Psychological Trauma: Theory, Research, and Policy, 1,* 114-124.

Gonzalez, A. (2018). Eye movement desensitization and reprocessing (EMDR) in complex trauma and dissociation: reflections on safety, efficacy and the need for adapting procedures. *Internal Society for the Study of Trauma and Dissociation, 2*(1), 192-211. https://doi.org/10.46716/ftpd.2018.0012

Granieri, A., Guglielmucci, F., Costanzo, A., Caretti, V., & Schimmenti, A. (2018). Trauma-related dissociation is linked with maladaptive personality functioning. *Frontiers in Psychiatry, 9*(206).

Guerin-Marion, C., Sezlik, S., & Bureau, J. (2020). Developmental and attachment-based perspectives on dissociation: beyond the effects of maltreatment. *European Journal of Psychotraumatology, 11*.

Hardy, A. (2017). Pathways from trauma to psychotic experiences: A theoretically informed model of posttraumatic stress in psychosis. *Hypothesis and Theory, 8*(697).

Helmes, E., Brown, J.-M., & Elliott, L. (2015). A case of dissociative fugue and general amnesia with an 11-year follow-up. *Journal of Trauma & Dissociation, 16*(1), 100–113. https://doi.org/10.1080/15299732.2014.969469

Hennig-Fast, K., Meister, F., Frodl, T., Beraldi, A., Padberg, F., Engel, R. R., Reiser, M., Möller, H.-J., & Meindl, T. (2008). A case of persistent retrograde amnesia following a dissociative fugue: Neuropsychological and neurofunctional underpinnings of loss of autobiographical memory and self-awareness. *Neuropsychologia, 46*(12), 2993–3005. https://doi.org/10.1016/j.neuropsychologia.2008.06.014

Holmes, J. (2017). Attachment, psychoanalysis, and the search for a 21st century psychotherapy practice. *Psychoanalytic Inquiry, 37*(5), 309-318.

Holmes, J. (2017). Roots and routes to resilience and its role in psychotherapy: a selective, attachment-informed review. *Attachment & Human Development, 19*(4), 364-381.

Huntjens, R. J. C., Wessel, I., Hermans, D., & van Minnen, A. (2014). Autobiographical memory specificity in Dissociative identity disorder. *Journal of Abnormal Psychology, 123*(2), 419-428.

Itzkowitz, S. (2015). The dissociative turn in psychoanalysis. *The American Journal of Psychoanalysis, 75*, 145-153.

Jacobson, L., Fox, J., Bell, H., Zeligman, M., & Graham, J. (2015). Survivors with Dissociative identity disorder: Perspectives on the counseling process. *Journal of Mental Health Counseling, 37*(4), 308-322.

Javinsky, T.-R., Udo, I., & Awani, T. (2024). Eye movement desensitisation and reprocessing: part 2 – wider use in stress and trauma conditions. *BJPsych Advances, 30*(4), 220–229. https://doi:10.1192/bja.2022.3

Jia, H. & Lubetkin, E. I. (2020). Impact of adverse childhood experiences on quality-adjusted life expectancy in the U.S. population. *Child Abuse & Neglect, 102*.

klein Selle, N., Ben-Shakhar, G., Kindt, M., & Vershuere, B. (2018). Preliminary evidence for physiological markers of implicit memory. *Biological Psychology, 135*, 220-235.

Lahav, Y., Ginzburg, K., & Speigel, D. (2020). Post-traumatic growth, dissociation, and sexual revictimization in female childhood sexual abuse survivors. *Child Maltreatment, 25*(1), 96-105.

Lawson, D. M., Stulmaker, H., & Tinsley, K. (2017). Therapeutic alliance, interpersonal relations, and trauma symptoms: Examining a mediation model of women with childhood abuse histories. *Journal of Aggression, Maltreatment & Trauma, 26*(8), 861-878. https://doi.org/10.1080/10926771.2017.1331941

Leonard, D. & Tiller, J. (2016). Dissociative identity disorder (DID) in clinical practice – what you don't see may hurt you.

Australasian Psychiatry, 24(1), 39-41.

Lesley, J. (2006). Awareness is relative: Dissociation as the organisation of meaning. *Consciousness and Cognition, 15*(3), 593–604. https://doi.org/10.1016/j.concog.2005.11.006

Lim, B. H., Hodges, M. A., & Lilly, M. M. (2020). The differential effects of insecure attachment of post-traumatic stress: A systematic review of extant findings and explanatory mechanisms. *Trauma, Violence, & Abuse, 21*(5), 1044-1060.

Lotfinia, S., Soorgi, Z., Mertens, Y., & Daniels, J. (2020). Structural and functional brain alterations in psychiatric patients with dissociative experiences: A systematic review of magnetic resonance imaging studies. *Journal of Psychiatric Research, 128*, 5–15. https://doi.org/10.1016/j.jpsychires.2020.05.006

Loewenstein, R. J. (2018). Dissociation debates: everything you know is wrong. *Dialogues in Clinical Neuroscience, 20*(3), 229-242.

Lynn, S. J., Lilienfeld, S. O., Merckelbach, H., Giesbrecht, T., & van der Kloet, D. (2012). Dissociation and dissociative disorders: Challenging conventional wisdom. *Current Directions in Psychological Science : A Journal of the American Psychological Society, 21*(1), 48–53. https://doi.org/10.1177/0963721411429457

MacIntosh, H. B. (2015). Titration of technique. Clinical exploration of the integration of trauma model and relational psychoanalytic approaches to the treatment of Dissociative identity disorder. *Psychoanalytic Psychology, 32*(3), 517-538.

Marais, L., Bezuidenhout, M., & Krüger, C. (2023). How do Patients

Diagnosed with Dissociative identity disorder Experience Conflict? A Qualitative Study. *Journal of Trauma & Dissociation, 24*(1), 125–140. https://doi.org/10.1080/15299732.2022.2119630

Marsh, R. J., Verschuere, B., Middleton, W., Dorahy, M. J., Butler, C., & Huntjens, R. J. C. (2018). Transfer of episodic self-referential memory across amnesic identities in Dissociative identity disorder using the autobiographical implicit association test. *Journal of Abnormal Psychology, 127*(8), 751-757.

Mauritzson, M., Bergendahl Odby, E., Holmqvist, R., & Nilsson, D. (2015). The fog is lifting; Veils of mist come and go: An interpretative phenomenological analysis of the experiences of six women recovering from pathological dissociation. *Journal of Interpersonal Violence, 30*(1), 45–61. https://doi.org/10.1177/0886260514532528

Meganck, R. (2017). Beyond the impasse – reflections on Dissociative identity disorder from a Freudian-Lacanian perspective. *Hypothesis and Theory, 8*(789).

Middleton, W., Sachs., A., & Dorahy, M. J. (2017). The abuse and the abuser: Victim-perpetrator dynamics. Journal of Trauma & Dissociation, 18(3), 249-258. https://doi.org/10.1080/15299732.2017.1295373

Morton, J. (2017). Interidentity amnesia in Dissociative identity disorder. *Cognitive Neuropsychiatry, 22*(4), 315-330.

Mosquera, D., Gonzalez, A., & Leeds, A. M. (2014). Early experience, structural dissociation, and emotional dysregulation in borderline personality disorder: the role of insecure and disorganized attachment. *Borderline Personality Disorder and Emotion Dysregulation, 1*(15).

Nguyen-Feng, V. N., Hodgdon, H., Emerson, D., Silverberg, R., & Clark, C. J. (2020). Moderators of treatment efficacy in a randomized controlled trial of trauma-sensitive yoga as an adjunctive treatment for posttraumatic stress disorder. *Psychological Trauma: Theory, Research, Practice, and Policy, 12*(8), 836–846. https://doi.org/10.1037/tra0000963

Nicholson, A. A., Densmore, M., Frewen, P. A., Theberge, J., Neufeld, R., McKinnon, M. C., & Lanius, R. A. (2015). The dissociative subtype of posttraumatic stress disorder: unique resting-state functional connectivity of basolateral and centromedial Amygdala complexes. *Neuropsychopharmacology, 40*, 2317-2326.

Nobakht, H. N. & Dale, K. Y. (2018). The importance of religious/ritual abuse as a traumatic predictor of dissociation. *Journal of Interpersonal Violence, 33*(23), 3575-3588.

O'Doherty, D. C. M., Tickell, A., Ryder, W., Chan, C., Hermens, D. F., Bennett, M. R., & Lagopoulos, J. (2017). Frontal and subcortical grey matter reductions in PTSD. *Psychiatry Research: Neuroimaging, 266*, 1-9.

Okano, K. (2018). The origin of so-called "shadowy personalities" in patients with Dissociative identity disorder. European Journal of Trauma & Dissociation, 3, 95-102. https://doi.org/10.1016/j.ejtd.2018.07.003

Orlof, W., Sołowiej-Chmiel, J., & Waszkiewicz, N. (2025). Selected aspects of diagnosis and therapy in Dissociative identity disorder (DID)-Case Report. *Journal of Clinical Medicine,*

14(8), https://doi.org/10.3390/jcm14082617

Paetzold, R. L., Rholes, S. W., & Andrus, J. L. (2016). A Bayesian analysis of the link between adult disorganized attachment and dissociative symptoms. *Personality and Individual Differences, 107*, 17-22.

Palmisano, G. L., Innamorati, M., Sarracino, D., Bosco, A., Pergola, F., Scaltrito, D., Giorgio, B., & Vanderlinden, J. (2018). Trauma and dissociation in obese patients with and without binge eating disorder: A case control study. *Clinical Psychology, 5.*

Paris, J. (2012). The rise and fall of Dissociative identity disorder. *The Journal of Nervous and Mental Disease, 200*(12), 1076–1079. https://doi.org/10.1097/NMD.0b013e318275d285

Perryman, K., Blisard, P., & Moss, R. (2019). Using creative arts in trauma therapy: the neuroscience of healing. *Journal of Mental Health Counseling, 41*(1), 80-94.

Peter, B. (2011). On the history of Dissociative identity disorders in Germany: The doctor Justinus Kerner and the girl from Orlach, or possession as an "Exchange of the Self." *International Journal of Clinical and Experimental Hypnosis, 59*(1), 82–102. https://doi.org/10.1080/00207144.2011.522908

Pica, M. (1999). The evolution of alter personality states in Dissociative identity disorder. *Psychotherapy, 36*(4).

Plokar, A., Bisaillon, C., & Terradas, M. M. (2017). Development of the child dissociation assessment system using a narrative story stem task: a preliminary study. *European Journal of Trauma & Dissociation, 2,* 21-29.

Raison, A., & Andrea, S. (2023). Childhood trauma in patients with

Dissociative identity disorder: A systematic review of data from 1990 to 2022. *European Journal of Trauma & Dissociation = Revue Europâeenne Du Trauma et de La Dissociation, 7*(1), 100310–100310. https://doi.org/10.1016/j.ejtd.2022.100310

Rasmussen, P. D. & Storebo, O. J. (2020). Attachment and epigenetics: a scoping review of recent research and current knowledge. *Psychological Reports, 0*(0), 1-23.

Raval, C. M., Upadhyaya, S., & Panchal, B. N. (2015). Dissociative fugue: Recurrent episodes in a young adult. *Industrial Psychiatry Journal, 24*(1), 88-90.

Rehan, M. A., Kuppa, A., Ahuja, A., Khalid, S., Patel, N., Cardi, F. S. B., Joshi, V. V., Khalid, A., & Tohid, H. (2018). The strange case of Dissociative identity disorder: Are there any triggers? *Cureus, 10*(7).

Reinders, A. A. T. S., Chalavi, S., Schlumpf, Y. R., Vissia, E. M., Nijenhuis, E. R. S., Jancke, L., Veltman, D. J., & Ecker, C. (2018). Neurodevelopmental origins of abnormal cortical morphology in Dissociative identity disorder. *Acta Psychiatrica Scandivavica, 137*, 157-170.

Reinders, A. A. T. S., Marquand, A. F., Schlumpft, Y. R., Chalavit, S., Vissia, E. M., Nijenhuism, E. R. S., Dazzan, P., Jancke, L., & Veltman, D. J. (2019). Aiding the diagnosis of Dissociative identity disorder: patters recognition study of brain biomarkers. *The British Journal of Psychiatry, 215*, 536-544.

Reinders, A. A. T. S., Nijenhuis, E. R. S., Quak, J., Korf, J., Haaksma, J., Paans, A. M. J., Willemsen, A. T. M., & den Boer, J. A. (2006). Psychobiological characteristics of Dissociative identity disorder: A symptom provocation study. *Biological*

Psychiatry (1969), 60(7), 730–740.
https://doi.org/10.1016/j.biopsych.2005.12.019

Ribary, D., Lajtai, L., Demetrovics, Z., & Maraz, A. (2017). Multiplicity: An explorative interview study of personal experiences of people with multiple selves. *Frontiers in Psychology, 8*(938).

Roelofs, K. (2017). Freeze for action: neurobiological mechanisms in animal and human freezing. *Philosophical Transactions, 372*(1718).

Romero-Lopez, M. J. (2016). A review of the dissociative disorders: from multiple personality disorder to the posttraumatic stress. *Anales de psicologia, 32*, 448-456.
https://dx.doi.org/10.6018/analesps.32.2.218301

Ross, C. A., Ferrell, L., & Schroeder, E. (2013). Co-occurrence of Dissociative identity disorder and borderline personality disorder. *Journal of Trauma & Dissociation, 15*(1), 79-90.

Sagan, O. (2019). Art-making and its interface with Dissociative identity disorder: No words that didn't fit. *Journal of Creativity in Mental Health, 14*(1), 23-36.

Sakae, K., Suka, M., & Yanagisawa, H. (2024). Dissociative identity disorder cotreated with Zinc and L-carnosine: A case report. *Curēus (Palo Alto, CA), 16*(11), e74794-.
https://doi.org/10.7759/cureus.74794

Santoro, G., Costanzo, A., & Schimmenti, A. (2019). Playing with identities: the representation of Dissociative identity disorder in the videogame "Who am I?" *Mediterranean Journal of Clinical Psychology, 7*(1).

Sar, V., Dorahy, M., & Krüger, C. (2017). Revisiting the etiological aspects of Dissociative identity disorder: a biopsychosocial perspective. *Psychology Research and Behavior Management, 10*, 137–146. https://doi.org/10.2147/PRBM.S113743

Sartory, G., Cwik, J., Knuppertz, H., Schurholt, B., Lebens, M., Seitz, R. J., & Schulze, R. (2013). In search of the trauma memory: A meta-analysis of functional neuroimaging studies of symptom provocation in posttraumatic stress disorder (PTSD). *PLOS ONE, 8*(3).

Saxena, M., Tote, S., & Sapkale, B. (2023). Multiple personality disorder or Dissociative identity disorder: Etiology, diagnosis, and management. *Curēus (Palo Alto, CA), 15*(11), e49057–e49057. https://doi.org/10.7759/cureus.49057

Schlumpf, Y. R., Reinders, A. A. T. S., Nijenhuis, E. R. S., Luechinger, R., van Osch, M. J. P., Jancke, L. (2014). Dissociative part-dependent resting-state activity in Dissociative identity disorder: A controlled fMRI perfusion study. *PLOS ONE, 9*(6).

Schroder, J., Nick, S., Richter-Appelt, H., & Briken, P. (2018). Psychiatric impact of organized and ritual child sexual abuse: cross-sectional findings from individuals who report being victimized. *International Journal of Environment Research and Public Health, 15*, 2417-2434.

Schweizer, S., Atzil, S., Hitchcock, C., Barrett, L. F., Satpute, A. B., Field, A. P., Black, M., & Dalgleish, T. (2019). The impact of affective information on working memory: a pair of meta-analytic reviews of behavioral land neuroimaging evidence. *Psychological Bulletin, 45*(6), 566-609.

Scimeca, G., Bruno, A., Pandolfo, G., La Ciura, G., Zoccali, R. A., & Muscatello, M. R. A. (2015). Extrasensory perception experiences and childhood trauma: A Rorschach investigation. *The Journal of Nervous and Mental Disease, 203*(11), 856–863. https://doi.org/10.1097/NMD.0000000000000381

Shatrova, D., Cáncer, P. F., & Caperos, J. M. (2024). The role of interoception in reducing trauma-associated distress: a feasibility study. *European Journal of Psychotraumatology, 15*(1). https://doi.org/10.1080/20008066.2024.2306747

Sierra, M., Medford, N., Wyatt, G., & David, A. S (2012). Depersonalization disorder and anxiety: a special relationship? *Psychiatry Review, 197,* 123-127.

Skałbania, J., Polewik, K., Pietkiewicz, I. J., & Tomalski, R. (2021). Divided mind – divided brain. The neurobiology of Dissociative identity disorder from the perspective of dynamical systems theory. *Psychiatria i Psychologia Kliniczna, 21*(1), 27–35. https://doi.org/10.15557/PiPK.2021.0003

Strouza, A. I., Lawrence, A. J., Vissia, E. M., Kakouris, A., Akan, A., Nijenhuis, E. R. S., Draijer, N., Chalavi, S., & Reinders, A. A. T. S. (2023). Identity state-dependent self-relevance and emotional intensity ratings of words in Dissociative identity disorder: A controlled longitudinal study. *Brain and Behavior, 13*(10), e3208-n/a. https://doi.org/10.1002/brb3.3208

Summit, R. C. (1983). The child sexual abuse accommodation syndrome. *Child Abuse & Neglect, 7,* 177-193.

Sutar, R & Chaturvedi, S. K. (2020). Symptom profile and diagnostic utility of depersonalization-derealization disorder: a retrospective critical review from India. *Indian Journal of*

Psychiatry, 62(1), 91-94,

Taïb, S., Yrondi, A., Lemesle, B., Péran, P., & Pariente, J. (2023). What are the neural correlates of dissociative amnesia? A systematic review of the functional neuroimaging literature. *Frontiers in Psychiatry, 14*, 1092826–1092826. https://doi.org/10.3389/fpsyt.2023.1092826

TeBockhorst, S. F., O'Halloran, M. S., & Nyline, B. N. (2015). *Psychological Trauma: Trauma, Theory, Research, Practice, and Policy, 7*(2), 171-178.

Terpou, B. A., Densmore, M., Theberge, J., Frewen, P., McKinnon, M. C., & Lanuis, R. A. (2018). Resting-state pulvinar-posterior parietal decoupling in PTSD and its dissociative subtype. *Wiley Periodicals.*

Thal, S. B., Daniels, J. K., & Jungaberle, H. (2019). The link between childhood trauma and dissociation in frequent users of classic psychedelics and dissocatives. *Journal of Substance Use, 24*(5), 524-531.

Trifu, S. (2019). Dissociative identity disorder. Psychotic functioning and impairment of growing-up processes. *Journal of Educational Sciences & Psychology, 9.*

van der Hart, O., Bolt, H., & van der Kolk, B. A. (2005). Memory fragmentation in Dissociative identity disorder. *Journal of Trauma & Dissociation, 6*(1), 55–70. https://doi.org/10.1300/J229v06n01_04

van der Hart, O., Nijenhuis, E. R. S., Solomon, R. (2010). Dissociation of the personality in complex trauma-related disorders and EMDR: Theoretical considerations. *J EMDR Pract and Res, 4*(2), https://doi.org.10.1891/1933-3196.4.2.76

van der Kloet, D., Merckelbach, H., Giesbrecht, T., & Jay Lynn, S. (2012). Fragmented sleep, fragmented mind: The role of sleep in dissociative symptoms. *Perspectives on Psychological Science, 7*(2), 159–175. https://doi.org/10.1177/1745691612437597

van der Kolk, B. A. (2003). The neurobiology of childhood trauma and abuse. *Child and Adolescent Psychiatric Clinics, 12*, 293-317.

Vermetten, E., Schmahl, C., Lindner, S., Loewenstein, R. J., & Bremner, J. D. (2006). Hippocampal and amygdalar volumes in Dissociative identity disorder. *The American Journal of Psychiatry, 163*(4), 630–636. https://doi.org/10.1176/appi.ajp.163.4.630

Vissia, E. M., Giessen, M. E., Chalavi, S., Nijenhuis, E. R. S., Draijer, N., Brand, B. L., & Reinders, A. A. T. S. (2016). Is it trauma-or-fantasy-based? Comparing Dissociative identity disorder, post-traumatic stress disorder, simulators, and controls. *Acta Psychiatrica Scandinavica, 134*, 111-128.

Webermann, A. R., Brand, B. L., & Chasson, G. S. (2014). Childhood maltreatment and intimate partner violence in dissociative disorder patients. *European Journal of Psychotraumatology, 5*(1), 1–8. https://doi.org/10.3402/ejpt.v5.24568

Wegen, K. S., van Dijke, A., Aalbers, A., & Zedlitz, A. M. E. E. (2017). Dissociation and under-regulation of affect in patients with posttraumatic stress disorder with and without a co-morbid substance use disorder. *European Journal of Trauma & Dissociation, 1*, 227-234.

Weniger, G., Lange, C., Sachsse, U., & Irle, E. (2008). Amygdala and hippocampal volumes and cognition in adult survivors of childhood abuse with dissociative disorders. *Acta Psychiatrica Scandinavica, 118*(4), 281–290. https://doi.org/10.1111/j.1600-0447.2008.01246.x

Wojciech, D. & Wojciech, L. D. (2016). Genetic and environmental basis of the relationship between dissociative experiences and Cloninger's Temperament and Character Dimensions – pilot study. *Polish Psychological Bulletin, 47*(4), 412-420.

More Than the Sum of Our Parts

www.ingramcontent.com/pod-product-compliance
Lightning Source LLC
Chambersburg PA
CBHW061728070526
44583CB00024B/3050